MW01029314

"Through transparent sharing, [...] yet rewarding realities of fostering [...] ous platitudes. No guilt-ridden ple. [...] t-by-moment dependence on the Lord through prayer is key to enabling a parent to go from strength to strength. Indeed, a much-needed resource for potential foster parents as well as a comfort for struggling parents. Highly recommended for DCS workers, social workers, and adoption agencies."

—SHERRIE ELDRIDGE, *author,* 20 Things Adopted Kids Wish *book series*

"*Faith & Foster Care* was a real 'shot in the arm' for me as I read it and reflected on my years as a foster parent. Reading so many real-life antidotes from others who shared many of the same experiences as my family was validation of our work, commitment, and the role our faith played in everything we did as foster parents. This is a must-read book for foster parents and other caregivers. It is honest about the challenges of fostering while speaking eloquently to the blessings it is to the foster parents, the children, and the birth parents of the children receiving foster care services. Job well done, Dr. DeGarmo, job well done."

—IRENE CLEMENTS, *executive director, National Foster Parent Association*

"*Faith & Foster Care* is truly an inspirational book directed toward the Christian foster parenting audience. The personal stories woven throughout the book from other foster parents make the book relatable and inspirational. Reading stories from those who have walked the faith-filled fostering journey provides a unique, profound voice to the book. The added Scripture passages help readers identify areas of the Bible that directly relate to foster care, adoption, and the call that many foster parents experience. This book is definitely ideal for those looking for a Christian-based perspective on foster parenting and a deeper, more inspirational look at how fostering impacts lives."

—KIM HANSEL, *editor,* Fostering Families Today *magazine*

"The Bible calls God's people to care for widows and orphans in their distress. This book is a helpful tool to move us from talk to action. For those who are opening their hearts and homes in foster care, Dr. John DeGarmo provides a guide to navigating the difficult issues and potential challenges that arise from this kind of ministry. I recommend this book for anyone considering answering God's call to care for these children in need."

—DANIEL DARLING, *vice president of communications for the Ethics and Religious Liberty Commission and author of* The Original Jesus

Faith & Foster Care

Dr. John DeGarmo

Faith & foster care

HOW WE IMPACT GOD'S KINGDOM

DR. JOHN DEGARMO

NEW HOPE
PUBLISHERS
Gospel-Centered. Missions-Driven.

BIRMINGHAM, ALABAMA

New Hope® Publishers
PO Box 12065
Birmingham, AL 35202-2065
NewHopePublishers.com
New Hope Publishers is a division of WMU®.

Library of Congress Control Number: 2016933810

Book design: Parapalla Design Shoppe

ISBN-10: 1-59669-472-6
ISBN-13: 978-1-59669-472-9
N164112 • 0516 • 2.5M1

For tiny Marquez,
who brought our family
hope, wonder, and love.

He has shown you, O mortal, what is good.
And what does the LORD require of you?
To act justly and to love mercy and to walk
humbly with your God.

—*Micah 6:8*

CONTENTS

I would like to thank God for His love and wisdom during my journey as a foster parent and for His guidance with this book. I would also like to thank Trish Heron for her help with the children as I wrote this book. Finally, thank you to all who contributed to this book with your personal stories. Each of you is not only an inspiration to many but also a light in the foster care world.

INTRODUCTION

My first exposure to what I would later learn had been foster care was to "go stay with" the nicest people I had ever met. That husband and wife were a wonderful couple who had lost their only child in a car accident. I don't remember their names or what they looked like. I don't know where they lived or anything else about them. But I vividly recall one conversation, one moment in time that changed me forever. The foster father told me that I was put here for a reason. Until then I believed that I was an accident of biology. Unwanted, unloved, "un-purposed." Although I couldn't have articulated it at seven or eight years old, I felt worthless and unworthy of the food I ate or the air I breathed. Suddenly, in one sentence, a person I liked and respected suggested that there was a purpose for my life.

The time I spent with those people was a time of firsts. It was the first time I'd been in a clean house. The first time I'd seen a shower. It was the first time I'd seen people eat with utensils. It was the first time I'd seen sheets and pillowcases and bedspreads that matched. It was the first time I could fall asleep knowing that I was perfectly safe. It was the first time I'd had plenty to eat. And it was the first time I met Jesus.

I was removed from that home because those lovely people took me to church. My atheist grandfather filed a complaint, and I never saw those people again, but the seed they planted in the brief time I was there took root. I was placed back in the custody of the abusive people from whom I'd been removed, and I lived in abuse and poverty until I emancipated at age 16. But the root of faith in Christ grew, and God made arrangements for me to stumble right into the purpose for which I was born, the purpose to which that foster father had alluded many years before.

Because of one brief conversation with one man, the entire trajectory of my life changed. Since 1989, I have dedicated my career to protecting the good people and organizations that help children who have been abused. And since the day I was baptized, July 4, 1976, I have done my best to fulfill the purpose for which I was born and perfectly matched, which is to help others find and fulfill God's perfect plans for their lives. Every good thing I'll ever do, every impactful word I'll ever speak, and every accomplishment I'll ever enjoy is because of those faith-filled people who took a dirty, difficult little girl into their home for a very short time.

No, I did not become a foster or adoptive parent. My career has been in the insurance industry, protecting and defending those who provide care to previously abused children. In that work, I see the selfless dedication of some of the most amazing people on earth to the care of other people's very wounded children. I call the challenge of raising children who often engage in very difficult behaviors "radical hospitality." Foster parents, the people I call "professional parents," are under-appreciated, underpaid, overworked, and often the subject of skepticism and even criticism related to motives for doing what they do. Family, friends, and neighbors often don't understand.

> **"** Loving a wounded child into wholeness is the most difficult, yet the most significant and rewarding, work anyone can do.

Christian foster parents changed the trajectory of my life and the lives of countless others. Every good thing anyone blessed enough to have a Christian foster parent will ever do is to the credit of the foster parent who shined the light of Christ into the darkness of a wounded child's soul. To love a broken child into wholeness is to achieve the ultimate success.

RHONDA SCIORTINO
Author of *Succeed Because of What You've Been Through*

CALLED TO FOSTER

*T*he urgency in my wife's voice was unmistakable. "John!" she called out to me, a second time. In my 14 years of marriage to my Australian bride, I had never heard such insistence in Kelly's voice, and I found it a little troubling.

"Coming," I said back to her. I was in the kitchen preparing dinner for the six children in our home while holding our newest foster daughter in my arms, who was screaming and using her small and fragile lungs to the utmost. The four-month-old infant, named Melinda, had done nothing but scream since she first arrived the day before, along with her four-year-old brother, Donnie. The tiny, underweight child was born addicted to the drug meth, our first experience with a meth-addicted child. My previous research had taught me that babies born to mothers addicted to meth generally suffer from a number of possible symptoms. Furthermore, I also found that these babies often suffer from brain damage, respiratory problems, neurological damage, organ damage, and general poor health. Melinda's nonstop screaming was probably due to the fact that the four month old was easily agitated, due to emotional problems, and sadly would most likely be for the rest of her life. Easily agitated. That would explain why she screamed, kicked, and fussed every waking moment. My heart had immediately broken when I found that this tiny little baby, innocent in all ways, suffered due to her biological mother's need to take the illegal drug. Handing her over to my 11-year-old daughter, I rushed into the bathroom, hoping to discover the cause of Kelly's distress.

When I arrived in our bathroom, I found my wife sitting next to the bathtub with tears streaming down her face. "What's wrong?" I promptly asked. During our years of marriage, and even before then during our time in the international performing group Up With People, where I first met Kelly as we traveled across the globe singing and dancing in front of thousands live and millions more on television, I had never seen her speechless before. Visibly upset, she had no words for me. Again I asked her, "What's wrong?"

As she tried to gather herself, Kelly pointed to the child's head, whereupon she feebly said between sobs, "Look."

Peering down at the four year old's blond hair, I was unable to see the cause of her concern. "I don't see anything," I replied.

Parting back Donnie's hair, my wife then repeated her earnest request: "*Look.*"

Looking down, I saw several tiny black circular marks on our foster son's head, marks I had not seen before, nor was certain of what they might represent. At first glance, they looked to be round burn marks, some fresh in appearance. "What are they?" I asked.

"Cigarette burns," my wife simply replied, wiping tears from her face. At this, I gasped in horror as the realization of what was before my eyes began to sink in. "Donnie, tell Mr. John how you got that booboo," she asked the child.

"That's where my mommy put her cigarettes when I get into trouble." He said it so matter of factly, as if it was a common occurrence, as if it was common practice for all adults when punishing their child.

Startled, I then asked, "Donnie, did your mommy put cigarettes anywhere else?" God, please no, I thought to myself.

"In here," the child said, opening his mouth wide and pointing to his tongue.

Bending over the tub, Kelly peered into Donnie's mouth. Shaking her head to indicate that there were some more burn spots on his tongue as well as the roof of his mouth, my wife quietly whispered to me, "She was probably trying to hide the evidence." Groaning in response, I could feel the anger begin to stir within me. This woman was his mother, the person who was supposed to keep him safe. This woman was the person who was supposed to protect him from anything that would harm him. How could she be so cruel? Staring down at him for a moment, my feeling of anger was swept away, and instead my heart began to fill with tenderness and compassion for the young child and for what he had been through. As Kelly began to help our foster son out of the bathtub, I walked back to the kitchen to resume dinner and retrieve a screaming Melinda from my daughter. Once again, I was reminded that there are so many children who need a foster home and so few homes willing to embrace these children. Fostering is a call, and God's call for families to take care of His children is clear throughout Scripture. To be sure, He wants families to take up His cross and look after His children in need.

A few months later, I attended my foster parent association's annual Christmas party, a time where the foster parents in my county gather together, along with our children (foster, biological, adoptive, and even some grandchildren sprinkled in there). It is a wonderful evening, with great food, fellowship, support, and even an appearance by Santa Claus with gifts for all the children. For all involved, it is a great way to spend the evening as we lift each other up in support and love.

I was able to spend some time chatting with a new set of foster parents who had recently joined our association. This loving husband and wife were parents to 12 children: biological, adoptive, and foster children. I was so impressed by their selflessness and dedication to children as they devoted their lives to helping them. Twelve children! I knew how tired they must have been. Recently, my wife and I had 11 children in our own home. Three of them were biological, three were adoptive, and the remaining five were foster children, a group of siblings that desperately needed a home. Our house was indeed a busy and crazy one, with children ranging in age from 18 months to 16 years, and everything in between. My wife and I knew little rest, and I am sure that this family was in much the same situation.

If truth be known, my wife and I both went to work to rest. Though her job as a massage therapist and doctor of nutrition kept my wife busy, as did my job as a media specialist and school librarian at the local high school in our small rural town of just over 2,000 people, we found the work as foster parents even more demanding. It seemed that when my wife and I both arrived home each evening, we were almost overcome by the mountains of laundry, dinner to cook for a small army, piles of dirty dishes, small children to bathe, homework with which to assist, and everything else that came along with a house full of children. Along with these tasks came trying to help our children from foster care face the daily challenges and traumas with which they struggled from the various horrors that brought them into the foster care system. By the time our heads hit our pillows late each evening, my wife and I were beyond tired, and sleep quickly overcame the both of us.

While traveling across the country working with thousands of foster parents at training conferences and speaking engagements, I continue to meet many such foster parents who are working tirelessly to help children in need. Over and over again, I am inspired by their stories of dedication, unconditional love, and servanthood. The foster parents I met in Texas who only care for babies who are dying from terminal illnesses are one example. They rock these babies in a chair until they die, making sure they are loved until their last breath. Another is the single foster father in South Carolina who only looks after troubled teenage boys. Yet another is the single foster mother in West Virginia who cares for young teenage girls and their babies. These are just a few of the inspirational people I have met through the years, all dedicating their lives to helping children in need and sharing God's love with them.

I have found that society at large does not really understand or appreciate what foster care is. They do not realize what foster children go through each day nor, for that matter, what foster parents go through. Even my own friends and family members do not fully understand what my wife and I experience each day as foster parents, or really why we do it. I even have family members who question why my wife and I continue to take into our hearts and home children who are in need after all these years of sleepless nights and stress-filled days. God's call on my life, though, is a strong one, and one that my wife and I cannot ignore, as I am sure it is for you as well.

Before I was a foster parent, I had some mixed views about the foster care system. To say that I was naïve and ignorant of what foster care is would be quite the understatement. I had two views of foster care. First, foster children were troublemakers, and it was their fault they were in the system. Second, foster parents were pretty weird people. Well, I got one thing correct: the second part. I was really wrong about the first part. Foster parents are pretty weird people, and I have been a foster parent for 12 years as I write this.

We have to be a little weird to do what we do, don't we? After all, foster parents dedicate their lives to serving other people by bringing into their homes and families children who are in need, children who are often troubled, and children who many times have a variety of challenges. To be sure, foster parenting is the hardest thing I have ever done, and continue to do. Perhaps this difficulty is why so few answer the call to be foster parents, as it is a job that requires a great deal of sacrifice from the parent(s) and from the rest of the family.

A successful foster parent is one who provides a caring environment while a birth family works on their caseload, the court-ordered responsibilities that are required for reunification, until the child and birth parent are reunited and living together once again. Foster parents not only provide a caring environment but a safe and stable one as well. During this time, foster parents agree to carry out all functions of the birth family. These day-to-day functions include assuring that the child's medical, nutritional, educational, and parental needs are met. Foster parents may also provide social activities for the child, such as extracurricular events after school, city and county sports, and church-related activities, to name a few. Without question, there can be much joy in being a foster parent. This joy comes from experiences like watching a child in foster care smile for the first time after years of abuse, teaching a child in foster care how to ride a bike, or sharing a foster child's first real birthday with him after so many birthdays have been ignored in the past.

As I wrote in my book *The Foster Parenting Manual*, "Foster parenting is hard work! . . . You will often find yourself exhausted, both mentally and physically . . . There is very little money available to help you, and you will not be reimbursed for all the money you spend on your foster child. The job will require you to work 24 hours a day, seven days a week, with no time off. You will probably feel overworked and underappreciated. You will work with children who are probably coming from difficult and harmful environments. Some of these children will have health issues, some will come with behavioral issues, and some will struggle with learning disabilities. Many times, the children you work with will try your patience and leave you with headaches, frustrations, disappointments, and even heartbreaks. There is a reason why many people are not foster parents, as it is often too difficult. The turnover rate for foster parents in the

United States is between 30 and 50 percent each year (U.S. Department of Health and Human Services 2005)."

There have been those moments when I have questioned whether or not I was making a difference. There have been those times when I have grown frustrated with the system, as I have had to stand by and watch some of the children in my home go back to environments and situations that I knew were not healthy or safe. I have also seen my wife's doubts and her desire to no longer foster as her heart has been broken numerous times as she has grown to love many children, only to see them return to homes where they were once again placed in jeopardy. It is the same for so many foster parents who have shared their stories with me. I have heard from foster parents who lose sleep each night for weeks and months on end, trying to calm and soothe a baby born addicted to crack, heroin, or meth. I have heard from foster parents who have been yelled at on a daily basis from foster teens who are so emotionally upset by their own experiences that they take it out on their foster parents. I have heard from those who have been told one day they could adopt their foster babies, only to be told another day that the baby would return instead to a biological family member the child had never met. The stories are countless, the stories are heartbreaking, and the stories are never ending. Surely, there is no earthly reason to be a foster parent. So, why do we do it? For many, like my wife Kelly and I, we are answering a call.

GOD'S CALL IS CLEAR

Remember Donnie? He had never known a safe parental love before coming to our home. For me and my wife, it was not only an opportunity to care for this suffering little child, but it was our responsibility as Christians to do so as well.

God's call for us to be foster parents is clear throughout Scripture as He tells us to take care of His children. Throughout this book, we will examine several verses in the Bible. First, let's look at Matthew 25:35–36 and see how it applies to foster children:

For I was hungry and you gave me something to eat, I was thirsty and you gave me something to drink, I was a stranger and you invited me in, I needed clothes and you clothed me, I was sick and you looked after me, I was in prison and you came to visit me.

Like me, you have probably witnessed many children coming into your home as foster children who fit this description. So many children in foster care come from homes that have no food or water. In fact, a number of children come into foster care who were previously homeless, either living on the streets and depending upon themselves, or living in a hotel room with parents who had no place of their own. Far too many children arrive into foster care with a lack of proper nutrition and a healthy diet. I remember one four-year-old boy who came to live with me. His name was Scotty. Scotty had a smile that could light up the darkest room, one that was so full of joy. Scotty's smile quickly endeared him to the members of my church, and he found a special place in their hearts. Yet all of Scotty's teeth were rotted out due to poor nutrition. At age four! All of his teeth! The four year old was terribly underweight and could speak only two words: "me hungry!" It was Scotty's battle cry. Everywhere the young foster child went, he would answer everyone's greeting with "me hungry." Three months after he came to live with us, Scotty had oral surgery and received a set of false teeth. Again, only four years of age, and yet he had been through so much trauma.

The foster child and the black plastic bag are often sadly linked together. Many times foster children will arrive at a foster parent's house with only the clothes on their backs, their only belongings. Others may come with their possessions in a black plastic bag, hastily gathered by the child's caseworker as he or she scurried to collect the few belongings together while an anxious biological mother plead for the child to remain with her. Quite recently, I listened to a foster parent who had a group of three siblings arrive at his home with only the clothes on their backs, clothes that were not only stapled together in some places but were so infested with human and dog feces that they had to burn the clothing before the children came into their home. Can you imagine? It literally makes my skin crawl to hear such stories.

And then there is the part of the verse where Jesus talks to His disciples about the sick. Children in foster care often come to our homes with a variety of illnesses—lice, scabies, and a host of other problems due to poor living conditions and neglect. Many times these children also suffer from mental health issues. These issues might include anxiety related disorders, reactive attachment disorder (RAD), anger issues, panic disorder, depression, and so forth.

To be sure, there are high levels of mental health problems with children under foster care.

God's call to us is clear. He is very concerned about those who are in need and commands us to care for them. He wants us to look after those who are sick and those who have no food or water. Nowhere in the Bible does it say that we will have an easy time doing it. Nevertheless, as followers of Christ, this care is what we are called to do. God tells us in the Old Testament that we are to care for those who are fatherless. Look at what else this verse says:

> LEARN TO DO GOOD; SEEK JUSTICE, CORRECT OPPRESSION;
> BRING JUSTICE TO THE FATHERLESS, PLEAD THE WIDOW'S CAUSE.
> —ISAIAH 1:17 (ESV)

According to The Annie E. Casey Foundation (aecf.org), there are roughly a half million children in foster care in the United States on any given day. These children are all children of God, and children who are hurting through no fault of their own. As foster parents, we can answer this call, as children are very important to Jesus. He points this importance out several times in the Bible. Jesus' view of children is both beautiful and specific, and one that we as foster parents need to remember. Consider these statements He made:

> AND HE TOOK A CHILD AND PUT HIM IN THE MIDST OF THEM,
> AND TAKING HIM IN HIS ARMS, HE SAID TO THEM, "WHOEVER
> RECEIVES ONE SUCH CHILD IN MY NAME RECEIVES ME, AND WHOEVER
> RECEIVES ME, RECEIVES NOT ME BUT HIM WHO SENT ME."
> —MARK 9:36–37 (ESV)

> WHOEVER RECEIVES ONE SUCH CHILD IN MY NAME RECEIVES
> ME, BUT WHOEVER CAUSES ONE OF THESE LITTLE ONES WHO BELIEVE IN ME
> TO SIN, IT WOULD BE BETTER FOR HIM TO HAVE A GREAT MILLSTONE FAS-
> TENED AROUND HIS NECK AND TO BE DROWNED IN THE DEPTH OF THE SEA.
> —MATTHEW 18:5–6 (ESV)

> THEN CHILDREN WERE BROUGHT TO HIM THAT HE MIGHT LAY
> HIS HANDS ON THEM AND PRAY. THE DISCIPLES REBUKED THE PEOPLE,
> BUT JESUS SAID, "LET THE LITTLE CHILDREN COME TO ME AND
> DO NOT HINDER THEM, FOR TO SUCH BELONGS THE KINGDOM
> OF HEAVEN." AND HE LAID HIS HANDS ON THEM AND WENT AWAY.
> —MATTHEW 19:13–15 (ESV)

In order to understand why Christians are called to foster children in need, as well as to appreciate how the Christian faith can help foster parents, I think it is important that we look at what foster parenting is, where it came from, and understand how the system works. First, let's start with a very short history of the foster care system in the United States.

Brief History of Foster Care

If you remember your history classes back in high school, you will remember that the early 19th century saw the establishment of the middle class. It was around this time that the idea began to form and grow that early childhood was an important and separate part of human development. New theories sprang forth, including the theory that internalizing beliefs of morality and behavior shapes a child's character. This theory was different than the colonial approach, which believed that a child's character was developed by first breaking their wills. As you can imagine, the outcome of this new method of rearing children was pretty spectacular. The result? Children began to live longer and stay home for longer periods of time instead of being forced to enter the workforce at early ages. It was around this time that some states were required to furnish children a minimum of three months of education per year. What is interesting to note is that religious institutions and charitable organizations began opening their own orphanages as churches and the like began to answer the call to help children in need.

In 1853, one man had a vision to improve the lives of children who were in desperate need of help, protection, and love. Charles Loring Brace, a stern and well-known critic of orphanages and asylums, introduced the idea of placing these children in homes rather than the traditional orphanage. (Remember the story of Oliver Twist? He was in an orphanage, and it was not so warm and caring of a place, according to the author, Mr. Charles Dickens.) Brace founded the Children's Aid Society (CAS) later in that year. It was his vision, and that of the CAS, that children should not be placed in institutions and orphanages but homes. Furthermore, it was Brace's personal belief that children should live in rural areas, as he was against city life. As a result, Brace endeavored to place children from urban slums into homes in the country.

Ever hear of Mary Ellen Wilson? I had not either until I did some research for my doctoral dissertation. I spent a full two years simply researching the history of foster care, and I stumbled upon Miss Wilson's name buried in the middle of a book somewhere. Mary Ellen Wilson is important to the foster care story. In 1873, Mary was a young girl, bruised, extremely skinny, and caked in dirt. She was also quite ill when a church worker found her, immediately began to care for her, and perhaps saved her life. When a New York judge became aware of the situation through neighbors of the church worker, Mary Ellen was removed from the church worker's home and was placed into another home, another house, and another family. Mary Ellen Wilson became the first official foster child.

Today's foster care system looks much different than it did in Brace's day. Today's foster care is a form of placement for children who need a home or environment outside of their home of origin. There are roughly 500,000 children in foster care in the United States on any given day. Of these 500,000, 25,000, on average, exit or age out of the system each year. The average amount of time a foster child spends in the foster care system is 28.6 months, with half of all foster children being placed in another home for a year or more (DeGarmo, 2015-Helping Foster Children in School, JKP). As a result, most of these children have not experienced a stable or nurturing environment during their early, formative years.

Placement in the foster care system today takes many forms. Some children may live in a foster home with foster parents unrelated to them. Other children may live with relatives temporarily or with family members intent upon adopting the child. This practice is commonly known as kinship care and is currently growing in popularity within the foster care system. Still, other foster children may reside within groups or even an intensive form known as Treatment Foster Care, which provides therapeutic treatment services. The end goal of foster care is for reunification, or reuniting, with biological parents or other family members. Sadly, this reunification is not always possible, and many children in foster care become eligible for adoption each year.

Deciding to Foster

In my book *The Foster Parenting Manual*, I shared the following information to help individuals make the decision to foster or not.

Making the decision to be a foster parent is a difficult one. It takes incredible commitment, unconditional love, and patience. After you determine that you are ready to begin, there are long hours of training ahead of you before your first foster child is placed in your home and becomes part of your family. These hours of training will go a long way in helping you prepare for the many challenges that await you as a foster parent.

Whether you are fostering in the United States or another country, each organization has its own set of laws and policies in regard to foster parent training. Thus, your situation will probably be different than somebody else who lives in a neighboring state. The first step is to locate your city's child welfare agency and contact them. Perhaps you already know someone who is a foster parent, and they can help you find the correct contact information. If so, you are one step ahead. If not, the phonebook or Internet is a great way to find [local resources]. As each state is different, you will find that there are a number of different names for child welfare agencies. [You will find in the appendix of this book a list of each state's child welfare agency and contact information.]

Before contacting the agency nearest to you, it is important to determine if you qualify as a possible foster parent, as there are requirements to be met before you become certified. These include the following:

AGE: Foster parents need to be at least 21 years of age in order to begin taking foster children into their homes.

CHARACTER: Character references are necessary in many occupations, including fostering children. You must have three signed statements from individuals stating that you have strong moral character, are able to develop meaningful relationships with children, can effectively manage financially, and have sound judgement.

FINANCES: Though you will be reimbursed for having a foster child placed in your home, the daily reimbursement fee is small and differs from state to state. Before a foster child is placed in your home, you may be asked to show that you are financially stable enough to support another child.

HEALTH: Having a foster child in your house can be draining, emotionally, mentally, and physically. In order to have a child placed in your home, each member of your family must be in mental and physical health. This includes no drug or alcohol abuse. You, and each member of your household, will have to have a medical examination, and a physical report from your doctor will have to be turned in to the child welfare agency, and kept on file.

MARITAL STATUS: As each state is different, your marital status may be a factor in your certification as a foster parent. If you are married, you will have to submit a copy of your marriage certificate to the child welfare agency and kept on file. If your status should change any time you are a licensed foster parent, you will have to report this change to your agency.

SUPERVISION: Foster parents are responsible for the whereabouts, care, and supervision of a foster child at all times. If you, and your fellow foster parent, are employed outside the house, plans for your foster child's supervision must be detemined prior to bringing a foster child into your home. Your child welfare agency will require prior approval for a child's supervision outside of your home, such as a daycare environment.

TRAINING: After contacting the agency in your city, you will begin the first phase of your training, the pre-service portion. In some states, this is known as the Model Approach to Partnership in Parenting, or MAPP, while other states refer to this first training as Parent Resource for Information, Development, and Education, or PRIDE. Both of these initial training sessions concentrate on delivering information in regard to the basic requirements you will need if you choose to become a foster parent. As you begin this training, your state's child welfare agency will ask you to perform two important tasks: a criminal background history and a home evaluation.

BACKGROUND CHECKS: Criminal background checks are mandated by all states when becoming licensed to supervise and care for foster children in your home. Both your state's criminal justice service and the Federal Bureau of Investigation (FBI) will need to obtain a set of fingerprints from you, as well as for each member of your household who is over the age of 18 years. Your fingerprints will be kept on file by the agency. If an arrest or conviction should appear on your background check, you will be unable to be licensed as a foster parent.

HOME EVALUATION: During a home evaluation, your house will be inspected to determine if it is well maintained and clean enough for a foster child to stay in. Along with this, the child welfare agency will also determine if the house is properly heated and plumbing is in order; if there are adequate sleeping arrangements for each child; if smoke detectors are in place and working; and if all medication and cleaning equipment are safely stored away.

Recently, a foster parent by the name of Melinda wrote to me sharing why she and her husband became foster parents.

MELINDA'S STORY

My husband and I have been fostering for 12 years now. We have adopted three children and have two foster children. I believe fostering is a calling from God and not something that everyone can do. I also feel strongly that He is very saddened by hurting children and even more so by people that are able to ease their pain and don't. I have been amazed over the years at how many times I thought I just couldn't do it anymore, and God somehow renews me and reminds me why I do.

We have two biological children, and I always knew I wanted at least four or more children. As they grew older, we didn't have any more children, and I had a bitterness about it. I actually privately held it against my husband and God. At the same time, I had a real guilt for feeling that way because I was blessed with two beautiful children and some people have none. Looking back, it was all so clear what He had planned, but I couldn't see it at the time. One day I was at the grocery store, and someone at the checkout commented on how tired she was after so many kids all day. We began talking, and I learned that she was a social worker for the Department of Social Services (DSS). This was all foreign to me, and I was full of questions.

Our son got a job at that same grocery store bagging groceries, and after a few weeks came home with an application to be a foster parent from the cashier. We looked it over and pushed it aside, not giving it much more thought. Then it seemed everywhere I turned I was hearing or reading something about foster care. One of my biggest complaints over the years has been that people don't know about or hear enough about foster care, but at that time in my life, foster care seemed to be everywhere and wouldn't leave me alone. That was definitely God working on me, but I didn't see it. He started sending these messages and wouldn't stop until one day I realized my anger and bitterness was completely gone, and I felt completely whole and content. At that point I realized the plan was there all along for my lifelong dream of many children. That has really helped strengthen my faith to be patient and know that His plan is always best. He does have a sense of humor because sometimes I feel like He is saying to me, "You want children? I'll give you children." With seven of them now, I keep telling Him I'm good, but I guess that's His decision, too.

I wouldn't change any of this, and I am really glad we didn't have more biological children, because foster children are already here and need parents, and He has given me and my husband, Charlie, the ability to love them all the same whether biological, adopted, or foster. Somehow over 12 years, everything we have needed has fallen into place and worked out. People tell us we are a blessing to these kids when truly we are the ones being blessed. My faith has taught me that it's not about me and that it's better for me to hurt than for a child to hurt. When I think about the hurt God suffered for us to be saved, then I can endure this pain for Him. Life could be a lot easier for us now, and we might even have more money if we hadn't started fostering, but I wouldn't change anything! I know this is what we are supposed to be doing.

Amen, Melinda. Amen!

CHAPTER 2

LIVING A LIFE OF FAITH
AS A FOSTER PARENT

For several years now, I have been accused of being crazy for taking so many children into my home. My workmates, friends, and even family members have told me countless times that I can't care for every child that comes into the foster care system. They tell me that I need to look after myself, that I might wear myself out, and that I won't be able to do the things that I want to do. There have even been those times when I have had close friends and family members shake their heads and sigh at me when I inform them that my wife and I have taken yet another child into our home. People often wonder why we do it, why we are foster parents. You probably get the same questions as well.

I need to be honest with you and tell you a little secret. Don't tell my wife that I am sharing this with you, OK? For the past six years, my wife Kelly has said the same thing every time a child leaves: "I am never doing this again." She is often quite adamant about it. She has told me this time and time again, sometimes quite sternly, sometimes with a fierce passion. She does not say it because being a foster parent is hard. No, she tells me this each time because, quite simply, it breaks her heart. Each time a foster child leaves our home, my wife breaks into tears, mourning the loss of a child that she has come to love. You see, when we take a foster child into our home, we not only provide a stable home and a family, we also love them

33

unconditionally. Kelly and I don't place labels on the children in our home. To us, there is no difference between a biological, adoptive, or foster child. They are our children, and we love them the same. So, when a child is moved from our home, it is often very difficult emotionally. Kelly often spends days in tears due to the loss of another child from our home. It is often said that a foster parent's heart is like a quilt with all the patches covering up the torn pieces.

As I write this chapter, my wife and I have taken in two more children in the past 36 hours. Now, allow me please to back up to just a week before. It was a Friday, and the 14-year-old foster son for whom we had been caring during the past year had just left our home. Though we found comfort in the knowledge that he was moving to a wonderful new home, we also grieved for the loss. Twelve months is a long time to have a child in your home, and we had come to love him like our son. My wife and I were both grieving the loss of our foster son when my wife looked at me with tears in her eyes and said, "I mean it, I am done with this. No more, I just can't take it." This time, I felt she really meant it, and it looked like our days of being foster parents were about over. We had been on quite the parenting ride for the past 12 years. In fact, we had not had a day's break from being foster parents for the past three years, as the house had been full with at least one foster child during that time. We were both looking forward to a little time to ourselves and needed a break. With Kelly's insistence that she did not just want a break but no longer wanted to foster, I was disappointed, as I still felt called to take care of these children of God. At the same time, I also understood Kelly's pain and heartbreak and would support her wherever the road might lead.

Yet God's call to my wife is a strong one, as it is to so many foster parents. It was only eight days later when we received a phone call from a caseworker asking if we would take in an eight-year-old boy for a week for respite care, as his foster parents were going out of the state suddenly to a funeral and were unable to take the child with them. After a prayer asking for God's wisdom and guidance, my wife and I agreed, with my wife noting, "It's just for a week, and that's it." When he arrived later that evening, I watched my wife spring into action. Kelly has a gift which few others are blessed with: a heart for loving children that is both amazing and inspiring as she comforts those who need it the most. She has the ability to make anyone around her feel so very special, as she devotes her entire attention to that person. When this little fella arrived, he was terrified and confused. He did not know who we were. To him, we were strangers, and he was once again being moved to a home that was not his own and living with people he had never met.

Imagine, if you will, being taken away from your mother and your father without any warning at all. Imagine being taken away from your siblings, pets, stuffed animals, and toys. Imagine being taken away from your bedroom, house, yard, and neighborhood. Imagine, too, being taken from all of your relatives, friends, classmates, and everything you know. In addition, after all of this disruption, imagine if you were suddenly thrust into a strange house with strange people and informed that this circumstance was your new home and new family for the time being. This experience was how it was for this little eight-year-old boy. Kelly's compassion for the child was evident right away as she placed her arm around him. "Hi, Michael, thank you for coming and staying with us for awhile. You're just going to be with us for a few days, OK?" she asked as he dug his face deeper into her waist. "Are you a little worried, honey? I bet you are. It can be scary. Don't worry, sweetheart, we're going to take care of you for a little bit, and then you can go back home." I could hear the emotion begin to swell in my wife's thick Australian accent as she wiped the tears away that were slowly trickling down Michael's face, our newest family member.

Later that night, we both tucked him into bed, with Kelly gently kissing his forehead. "Kel, you are so good with him. You really do make our foster children feel a little better during these rough nights," I told her, my own voice choking with some emotion. My heart had already gone out to the child.

"Thanks, but I am not doing this permanently," she replied with a sad smile crossing her lips.

Yet when the phone rang the next day about taking in a newborn baby, my wife once again answered God's call to look after His children. This time, it was for a premature baby born at only 30 weeks and weighing all of two pounds. When I finished my conversation with the caseworker, I called Kelly, who was running some errands in town, and shared the information with her. After five weeks in the hospital, the baby boy was now five pounds and ready to be discharged to a foster family. The birth parents were both 19 years old, and the mother already had an earlier child placed with a foster family the year before. Furthermore, the birth mother was a former foster child herself and had only recently aged out of the foster care system. Sadly, she had been adopted and then given back to the state by her adoptive family.

"What do you think?" Kelly asked me. "Are we crazy?"

"Yes, we are. But, this is a child in need," I replied back to her. We then prayed about it, seeking God's guidance in taking another child into our home. After we finished, I then asked Kelly, "So, what do you think?"

"We are crazy," she reassured me. "So much for having some time to ourselves; can you call the caseworker and tell her we can take him?" I assured her that I would, though I did not remind her of her previous vow to no longer foster. Clearly, Kelly felt God's call strongly in her heart to live a life of faith and take care of the very least of these.

CHOOSING TO LIVE A LIFE OF FAITH

A few years ago, I asked a group of foster parents at a conference why they became foster parents. The answers I received did not surprise me as so many of them echoed my own reason. The majority to whom I spoke on that afternoon told me that they felt called by God to look after His children. For them, like so many others, foster parenting was simply answering God's call and living a life of faith that demonstrated God's love for all.

When a relative of mine asked me why I was so tired, I smiled and told them that sometimes it can be a little exhausting caring for seven children. With a look of non-approval, she then responded and told me that it was our choice and that we did not have to do it. At that time, I had three biological, one adopted, and three foster children. Our adopted child and the three siblings in foster care were all in diapers. You can imagine what our mornings were like as my wife and I tried to get all seven children ready: breakfast, changing diapers, feeding babies with bottles, getting the older ones ready for school, and trying to make sure that my wife and I both looked presentable when we went to work.

My relative was quite correct when she said that I had made a choice. To be sure, foster parenting is a choice, a voluntary act, if you will. Foster parents volunteer as an act of service to a child welfare agency or government organization. What many outside of foster care do not appreciate, though, is that foster parents have very little say in regard to the child's life. The agency or organization that has placed the child in the foster parent's home has control over every key area and decision regarding the child. We are choosing to take care of children that are not ours and doing so in a selfless manner. Sometimes these children might keep us awake at night, sometimes they might challenge us, sometimes they might resist our attempts to care for them, sometimes they might even fight us. It can be a daunting and difficult task at times. Goodness knows it has been for me on several occasions. Nevertheless, these children need us to care for them. One of my favorite hymns we sing in our church is the old classic "Here I Am, Lord," by Dan Schutte. Each time we sing it, the words penetrate me deeply, and I often have to swallow back the tears that threaten to replace my singing with sobbing. This hymn, first written in 1981, addresses God's call to look after children and hold these young people of His in our hearts. Just sharing the chorus alone with you brings a lump to my throat.

Here I am Lord. Is it I Lord?
I have heard You calling in the night.
I will go Lord, if You lead me.
I will hold Your people in my heart.

IRENE'S STORY

When my husband and I married, we knew we both wanted to have a large family. We assumed, as most people do, that we would be able to have children in the traditional manner, and after we were married for two years, we made the decision to begin that process. After three miscarriages, it became apparent that our plans for a large family were not to be.

We went to medical specialists and tried the current methods, at that time, to help us have a baby, but nothing worked. For the first time in my life, I began to question my faith. I stopped going to church regularly and stopped teaching Sunday School and doing other things at our church. I was feeling sorry for myself. One day about six weeks into my pity party, I walked by the bookshelf that held my Bible, and I had an overwhelming urge and need to open my Bible. I walked on by. But shortly, that overwhelming urge hit me again, and I gave in. I randomly opened my Bible. One verse stood out, almost as if it were the only verse written on those two pages. After I read that verse, I knew my Lord and Savior was indeed in control and that I was going to have my large family.

What verse did I read? What changed my life? It was Psalm 113:9, and it said, "He settles the childless woman in her home as a happy mother of children. Praise the LORD." I fell to my knees in thanksgiving and cried my heart out that day.

The rest is history. We applied to adopt a baby and were told it would be at least a two-year wait. Not so. That call came in six months, and we adopted our first child, a beautiful baby girl. After that, we applied to become foster parents, and over our 27 years of fostering, we adopted three more incredible children—two boys and another girl. We fostered 127 children, some of whom are still part of our family today.

Whenever we struggled with the foster care system, the extreme needs or behaviors of the children placed into our care, the concerns about what fostering was doing to our children, and so much more, all I had to do was revisit the last verse of Psalm 113 to fall to my knees and thank God for His many blessings.

LIVING OUR FAITH

God calls His people to display their faith in Him on a daily basis and in all that we do. This display of faith means to demonstrate His love in our actions. One way we can reveal our faith is by living out James 1:27, which tells us, "To look after orphans and widows in their distress and to keep oneself from being polluted by the world."

While not orphans, foster children surely do fit this Scripture, and many faith-based foster care organizations use this verse as their mission statement. God has placed within us a call to ease the suffering of children who are in need. Certainly, as ambassadors of Jesus Christ, we must stand up for children, these helpless and defenseless children, as Jesus would do for us. Think of it as an expression of our love for God, living the faith of Christianity in our actions. God is love, and for us to live for God, we need to live for love. To be sure, one way to live for love is to show this love in our actions, our beliefs, our thoughts, and our words. Bear in mind the words of 1 John 4:8:

WHOEVER DOES NOT LOVE DOES NOT KNOW GOD, BECAUSE GOD IS LOVE.

We live out a life of faith by loving others, even if they might not be able to return that love to us. If we are to obey the two greatest commandments as instructed to us in Matthew 22:37–40, then we are to love God and to love our neighbor. Is this calling easy? Well, for me, it is often not. I am quite flawed, and I sin several times each day, both in thought and deed. There are those days when I become frustrated with the foster care system and those in it. There are days when I become judgmental toward the birth parents of my foster children, even growing angry at some of them for the pain, suffering, and torture that some of these parents have given their children. I have had so many children in foster care come to live in my home who have been victims of rape, sexual abuse, neglect, and other horrors at the hands of those who were supposed to love and protect them the most: their birth parents and biological family members. I admit to you that there are moments when I harbor anger and resentment toward these family members. I realize, though, that these feelings of mine are wrong, as I have sinned just as much, in different ways. We know from Scripture that no sin is greater than another, and none is larger than my own.

Yet I am also reminded in these times that God has forgiven me for my sins and that He has taught me some amazing lessons of forgiveness, grace, and mercy in my own life. Just as God has forgiven me, I need to forgive others. Just as God loves me, unconditionally, and with all my warts and faults, I am called to do the same toward those who neglect or abuse their own children. Certainly, I am not to look at these people as enemies but as children of God, just as I am, children who also need both my love and His love. By showing our love for others, we can show God's love for others. This unconditional love allows us to show God's unconditional love for all of us, for when we love others, even those who are incapable of returning love, we are acting as a witness to how God loves each of us. To be sure, God commands us to look after these children. His words are quite clear in Psalm 82:3–4:

GIVE JUSTICE TO THE WEAK AND THE FATHERLESS;
MAINTAIN THE RIGHT OF THE AFFLICTED AND THE DESTITUTE.
RESCUE THE WEAK AND THE NEEDY;
DELIVER THEM FROM THE HAND OF THE WICKED. (ESV)

Rescue the weak and the needy, and deliver them from the hand of the wicked. Do these words ring true to you? Do these words speak about foster children? They certainly do to me. Children in foster care are weak. Children in foster care are needy. Most importantly, children in foster care need to be rescued. This rescue is what foster parents do; we rescue them by providing a safe and stable home. We clothe and feed them. We provide clean beds and a safe environment. And, perhaps most importantly, we love them. We are to love them as God would have us do for His "weak and needy."

CALLING PEOPLE OF FAITH

Recently, a foster parent shared her thoughts on foster care with me. She wrote to me in an email the following words:

> *The Christian faith calls people who feel God's love pulling at their heartstrings when they see children in need, and as the Bible instructs us, we are to reach out to His little ones. That calling is an awesome calling, I know because I am a Christian who was fostered for 15 years prior to getting into this ministry of being a foster parent. I have always believed that the eyes of a child are the windows to their souls. There are two moments you will never forget as a foster parent. The first is when you see that hurt, bewildered, sad-beyond-measure look in the eyes of a little child. The second moment you will never forget as a foster parent is when you look into the eyes of a precious little one and see happiness, trust, and love, and know that God has put that new view of their world through His love and your life through Christ. The eyes are the windows of the soul; that is a true statement.*

JILLIAN'S STORY

After finding out my husband and I couldn't have children, I dealt with depression for almost two years. I just didn't understand why some people could have "oops babies," but those ready to take full responsibility with a strong desire to have children couldn't. What did we do wrong in His eyes? I went about my daily life as a zombie, and once behind closed doors, I was a sobbing mess, yearning for a purpose. Over time, my heart slowly led me back to God, and I began to give my all to Him. After all, He is the one with the plan for me. He is the one that knows what my future holds, and when I stop trying to control it, that's when God's path for me is often shown. My husband and I then started searching for alternative routes to have children fill our home.

I didn't know anything about fostering but made a call to our local child welfare government agency, hoping to find out information. The woman that answered was so excited to hear from me and took my information right away to get a packet sent out in the mail. It was not even 15 minutes later when she called our house back. She told me that the last session of foster parent training for the year was scheduled to start in two weeks; they hadn't received the budget for the next year, so she wasn't sure when another one would start, and she wanted to know if we wanted to sign up. I quickly hopped online to find out what the training even was and called my husband. Two weeks later we started our training. What better way to do God's work and fill the hole I had in my heart than to help children in need.

We had a placement call just three weeks after being licensed, but at the last minute, that newborn was placed with his grandmother. We then carried on with our lives for another three months or so. I can remember like it was yesterday sitting in church on a Sunday, and the service was about being a godly parent. I sat and listened with full attention as I fought back tears. About 20 minutes into it, I looked at my husband, burst into tears, and told him I had to leave. I agreed with the teaching and wanted to learn more, but I just couldn't do it that day. Was our day ever going to come? That very same week, just days later, we received our first placement! That service about being a godly parent was just for us. That was our sign it was our time. What a fantastic rollercoaster ride we jumped on to! Within one hour of receiving the call, we suddenly had not one but two children in our car on the way home with us. They were an emergency removal case and came from abuse and neglect. The Department of Human Services informed us that they both had extreme cases of lice and had been given makeshift baths in the sink at the office.

We had no idea what we were walking into! They were scared, hungry, and filthy because of abuse and neglect, and they had a lot of issues we were soon to learn of. Neither of them knew how to talk, and they were two days away from being two years old. He was extremely aggressive, and she had very low self-esteem and was terrified of men. I suddenly was becoming concerned but determined to figure out how I was going to help these poor babies!

It took a while for things to get through the system, but with persistence and a lot of phone calls, help was well on its way! I set up doctors' appointments to discuss how to get them healthy (they were both underweight, she in the third percentile) and with a psychologist so I could learn how to help them cope with issues. We were then referred to Early On Head Start to help their development. At age two, they registered at the development of a 6–9 month old. We were all putting in a lot time and hard work and were seeing great improvements fairly quickly. They were moving mountains, to speak! As our first court date approached, I was curious as to what the biological parents' story was. Once we got to know a little information, I knew in my heart I was right where God wanted me to be, and that made me work even harder for these babies! The state gave the biological parents the benefit of the doubt, handed them everything that they needed, and gave them chance after chance after chance. I was so sad for them and for the twins that the parents just couldn't get it together. As much as I wanted to turn up my nose at these people that did awful things to innocent children, the Christian woman in me kept praying for them. I didn't understand how they could not have a bond with their children, how they couldn't care, how they couldn't want to better themselves for the twins. The thought of adoption was becoming more of a reality.

Fast-forward a year and a half. I found myself in termination court. Their biological mom didn't even show up, and their biological dad left halfway through the hearing. As termination was granted, I shed a lot of tears, tears of joy for the twins, their future, and the thought of becoming an official family, but also tears of sadness for the biological parents. We were referred to an adoption agency and were an official, legal family within four months (the fastest adoption case our worker had ever been a part of).

Through this journey I can truly and wholeheartedly say that I now know that everything happens for a reason. The good, the bad, and the ugly! I did not understand the purpose of my life just a few years ago, but once I gave it all to God and had faith and full trust in Him, the puzzle pieces started to fit together. I know I'm doing exactly what He wants me to do. It has been one heck of a ride, but I give all the glory to Him. The ride isn't over yet . . . just a few new chapters have begun!

DEFENDING THE
LEAST OF THESE

I am sure you have probably heard the popular tale of the starfish. The author is unknown, yet it is told often. The first time I heard it, I was spending a week just south of the border of Texas working alongside members of my church as we built basic housing for the people of Mexico. The story has stuck with me for several years since that long ago summer in 1999 as Kelly and I have welcomed more than 45 children in our home. Allow me, please, to share the story with you:

A man and his son were on a family vacation at the beach. The night before, there had been a fierce and terrific storm, one that lasted for hours. The howling wind and pounding waves had battered the surf long into the night and into the early morning. It was a frightening storm, and it had wreaked havoc on the beach. Now, hours later, the boy was curious what the storm had wrought and asked his father to take him for a walk. When they stepped onto the beach just as the sun was rising, they were immediately met with thousands of starfish littering the beach. The sea creatures had been washed up onto the shore from the brutal storm and lay across the sands in both directions for as far as both the father and son could see. Thousands upon thousands met their eyes, far too many to count. Soon after the two began walking on the wet sands, the boy bent down and picked up a starfish, throwing it far into the ocean. After doing so, he then bent down and picked up another one and threw that one into the water as well. This pattern went on for quite some time; the young boy threw starfish after starfish back into the ocean. After watching his son for some time, the father was confused about what his son was hoping to accomplish and finally asked, "Son, what are you doing?"

"I'm throwing these starfish back into the ocean," the young boy answered.

"I see. Tell me, please, why are you doing this?" the father continued questioning.

"Well Dad, the storm has washed all of these starfish onto the beach last night, and they can't return to the ocean by themselves," his son responded. "When the sun comes out and starts warming up the beach, the starfish will all die. They won't have oxygen and won't survive. The sun will also make it too hot for them. I have to throw them back into the water." As he said this, he continued picking up the starfish and throwing them back into the water.

"But son," the father said, sweeping his hand in the direction of the starfish all around him, "you can't possibly save all of these starfish. Just look, there are hundreds and thousands of them along the beach. It's useless. You can't possibly make a difference."

The boy stopped for a moment to take in his father's words. Frowning, he looked down at the starfish around his feet. Then, the boy bent down and picked up another starfish in his hand before throwing it as far as he could back into the ocean. Turning to his father with a large grin spreading across his face, he simply said, "It made a huge difference for that one!"

There are thousands of children in foster care. In the small county in which I live, each foster home is overflowing with foster children. Just a few months ago, we had 11 children in our home. That's right; you read correctly, that was 11 children. We had our three biological children, three adoptive children, and a sibling group of five foster children. Like most states, my current home state of Georgia has a limit of six children—including biological, adopted, and/or foster children—in a foster parent's home. Yet there are not enough foster homes, so waivers are signed, and we can take extra children if the need should arise.

So why do we continue to foster? Why, when our house is already full? It's really quite simple, and I am sure you feel the same way. When the phone rings, and the caseworker tells us that there is a child in need, we answer the call. As my own family has pointed out to me on a few occasions, I cannot save every child. But to be sure, I can help some, and so can you. Foster parents do make a difference. You are making a difference every time a foster child is placed in your home. You are making a difference every day a child is living with you. You are changing the life of a child. You are giving hope to a child, and you are giving that child a better future, just as God calls you to do. Recall the words of Jeremiah 29:11, which states:

> *"FOR I KNOW THE PLANS I HAVE FOR YOU," DECLARES*
> *THE LORD, "PLANS TO PROSPER YOU AND NOT TO HARM YOU,*
> *PLANS TO GIVE YOU HOPE AND A FUTURE."*

Hope. A future. As a foster parent, you have the potential of bringing a future of hope to a child. Of course, you cannot do so by yourself. God can work through you to change a life. God can use you to help bring hope to a child. We are simply answering God's call to do His work.

Did you know that many children in foster care have never had a birthday celebrated in their name? Are you aware that hundreds of thousands of foster children have never had a present to open on Christmas Day? This reality alone makes me sad. To think that a child is sitting in a home, right now, on his birthday, and there is no one who will sing "Happy Birthday" to him, no cake or ice cream party, no presents with his name on them, no one to make him feel special. Every child deserves to have his birthday celebrated. Every child deserves to have "Happy Birthday" sung to him.

I witnessed something like this recently. We had a child in our home, Andrew, who, along with his two other siblings, had come from a house of horrors. His mother was a meth addict, his father was never in the picture, and his house had no electricity, no food, no water, no plumbing, no heat, and no air. Furthermore, the entire floor of the house was covered in both dog and human feces. The child was seldom in school and had never truly been raised by his mother, as she was too often focusing her concerns upon her drug addiction. Andrew had a number of emotional challenges, including suffering from reactive attachment disorder (RAD), a condition in which children have great difficulty in forming healthy attachments with others. Far too many children in foster care are diagnosed with RAD, and they struggle mightily to connect with others on any type of social level. Children who are diagnosed with RAD also find it very difficult to keep their emotions in control. Andrew was often full of rage and was openly defiant at times, while at other times he was considerate and well-mannered. We never really knew when he might explode into rage as many things triggered his unleashed fury and anger.

Four months after his arrival into our home, Andrew's eleventh birthday rolled over on the calendar. As we do for everybody in our house, we celebrated his birthday in a large way. First, we woke him with breakfast in bed with his favorite cereal and a glass of orange juice, and all in the house surrounded him singing "Happy Birthday." I was a little surprised when his older brother and sister told me that they didn't know the words to the classic and familiar song. We then gave him one present to open that morning, with the rest to follow in the afternoon after school with cake and ice cream. When Kelly placed Andrew's present in front of him wrapped in colorful and festive wrapping paper, our foster son simply stared down at it, then to us, and then back to the present. "What is it?" he asked. With smiles on their faces and laughter in their voices, our own children then encouraged him to open it. Looking down at it with a confused look, Andrew simply sat in his bed turning the present over and over in his hands. Turning to my wife, the 11-year-old said, "I don't know how."

> For this child, the celebration of his birthday meant so very much to him and will be something he will remember for a long time to come. Such a simple gesture, the gesture of a birthday celebration, can be a tremendous healing opportunity for a child who has known no love in his life.

He didn't know how. An 11-year-old boy did not know how to open a present. Can you imagine? He had never had a present to open before. Not on his birthday, not on a holiday. No one to tell him how special he was on the day he was born, and how much he mattered on the day that was supposed to be celebrated in his honor.

For this child, the celebration of his birthday meant so very much to him and will be something he will remember for a long time to come. Such a simple gesture, the gesture of a birthday celebration, can be a tremendous healing opportunity for a child who has known no love in his life. After all, every child deserves to have "Happy Birthday" sung to him. Every child deserves to have a birthday party in his honor. Every child deserves the chance to blow out candles on his day. Birthdays should be a day of joy and hope for children. Sadly, for many it is a day that is ignored, a day that is forgotten, and a day that brings sadness and pain.

SAVING A CHILD FROM A DANGEROUS SITUATION

Children are placed into foster care for a variety of reasons. These may include neglect, physical abuse, sexual abuse, parental or adult drug and alcohol abuse, drug and alcohol abuse by the children themselves, domestic violence, inadequate housing or homelessness, abandonment, incarceration of a caretaker, or even death of a parent or family member. For whatever reason, hundreds of thousands of children each year need to be rescued from these dangerous situations and escape these homes of horror.

During my years as a foster parent, I have been witness to some true horror stories, horror stories that were all too real for innocent children. A few years ago, some friends of mine by the name of Linda and Kerry were taking care of two small children, both of whom had been exposed to acts of extreme neglect and violence. The oldest child in their home was an 18-month-old girl named Suzie whose mother was an unemployed teenager living off welfare. Little Suzie was born with an ailment that resulted in her having poor vision. In order to help correct the vision problem, the young mother was simply to place one drop into each eye, once a day. This care was all, just two drops total, once a day. Instead, the teenage mother would sit on the couch, watch television, and neglect the child and the drops. By the time my friends had the tiny, underweight, and malnourished child placed into their home, little Suzie was already legally blind and would never regain her sight. When I saw Suzie the first time, I was struck by the size of her large pupils. They resembled those of an owl: large brown pupils staring out sightlessly. Her foster parents informed me that Suzie's eyes had tried and failed to adjust to her weakening vision. As a result of her mother's negligence, little Suzie would never see again. What angered me the most was that this blindness could have been so easily prevented. The simple action of placing the eye drops into the child's eyes would have been one that would have required just a few seconds from the mother.

The other child's story is even more disturbing. Six-month-old Micah was placed into Linda and Kerry's home after suffering both tremendous pain and trauma. Little Micah's mother was living with her boyfriend, who had a history of domestic violence. One afternoon, after an argument with the baby's mother, the boyfriend decided to take out his anger on the helpless child and dipped his body into a pot of boiling hot water that was sitting on top of the stove. After taking him out of the boiling water, Micah's mother placed her son into his crib in another room. For the next 24 hours, Micah screamed in agony as his tiny body was wracked with such pain, his skin melting away from his body. It was only after his mother realized that her son would not quiet down that she took him to the hospital, 24 hours later. The damage had been done, though, to the defenseless infant. After numerous surgeries and several skin grafts, which did not succeed, little Micah was placed into my friend's home with both his legs in casts. Doctors tell Linda and Kerry that their foster son will most likely never be able to walk.

For both Micah and Suzie, the damage has been done, and they will suffer for the rest of their lives from the atrocities committed against them. Yet now they are both in a home that will protect them from further cruelty and neglect and are with people who will take care of them and love them. Linda and Kerry are a wonderful family who feel called by God to take care of foster children. These two have opened their hearts and home to children in need in such a way as to put their faith in action as they display God's mercy and compassion to both Micah and Suzie, and to all the other foster children God brings to them.

The Horrors of the Human Sex Trafficking Market

One of the most disturbing trends in foster care today is the ensnarement of thousands of young children in foster care into the dangerous world of exploitation, slavery, and sex trafficking, a world about which few in society know, and even fewer are fighting to bring to an end.

As you know, your foster child has one true wish and one real desire, more than anything else, and that wish is to be loved. As foster parents, we can protect the child from harm, provide a safe and secure home, offer nutritious meals, and open a doorway of opportunities, granting them new and exciting experiences of which they may never have dreamed. Yet with all of these gifts, with all of the wonderful opportunities and safe environments, foster children really crave love the most. They want to be loved, and they need to be loved. After all, every child deserves to be loved. Not only do children deserve love, they need it in order to grow in a healthy fashion. The greatest gift you and I have been given is love, a gift to us from God. He calls us to love one another, just as He loves us. While there are many forms of love, the strongest one, and most important for a foster child, is that of unconditional love. Sadly, many children in foster care either do not receive this love at all, or receive it too late, after too much emotional damage has been done.

Unconditional love is simply being loved without restrictions or stipulations. Jesus Christ loves us despite our many sins, and died for our sins upon that Cross more than 2,000 years ago. This sacrifice is a wonderful gift. We are all born sinners, and as humans each of us continues to sin in a variety of ways. There are days when I feel that I have not done a very good job in glorifying God and showing His love to others. Some days, I am not the best husband, other days I am not a good friend, while still other days I may not be the best foster father. Yet I am comforted with this fact: each morning I wake up white as snow, ready to start my day as a servant of God. As I go throughout each day, I unfortunately commit various sins, with each sin cutting into me and staining me with red. Yet, with God's grace and forgiveness, my sins are forgiven. How amazing!

For a foster child who may have been abused, beaten, or neglected, this type of unconditional love is most important, yet probably unknown. Your love as a foster parent is quite essential to the child's health, well-being, and future. Without this type of love, a love that does not judge and is forgiving, a foster child will not form necessary and healthy attachment with others, resulting in a number of attachment disorders. Foster children who suffer from these disorders will have great difficulty connecting with others as well as managing their own emotions, not only during their childhood and time in foster care but many times throughout the remainder of their lives. Emotional difficulties such as a lack of self-worth, lack of trust, and the need to be in control often result from the lack of unconditional and healthy parental love

A dark secret in America today is the prevalence of human sex trafficking. Many in society either are not aware of it or refuse to acknowledge its existence in our nation and around the world. It is emerging more each year as an area of grave concern for law enforcement and legal professionals, as well as those who work with social services, particularly those who work with foster children. Shockingly, between 300,000 to 400,000 children are exploited commercially in our nation for purposes of sex each year, many of these children being shipped, or trafficked, across international borders. For these thousands of children, a life of horror and danger is forced upon them as they serve as prostitutes for local and global criminal organizations. Thousands of children are sold into slavery by those who profess to love them the most: their family members. How large is the problem? Disturbingly, human trafficking generates more than $32 billion a year, which is second only to drug trafficking. Roughly 2 million children are exploited in this manner across the globe.

The average age of an American girl entering into sex trafficking is 13 years old. As a father of five girls myself, this fact disturbs me tremendously. Senator Amy Klobuchar of Minnesota put it wisely when she said, "They're not even old enough to go to a prom, not even old enough to get a driver's license and yet we still are seeing more and more of it on the Internet." The number of children being contacted by sexual predators online is disturbing and astounding at the same time. Approximately one out of every seven children is sexually contacted, or solicited, by a predator while online. Furthermore, many of these children are seriously pursued online by these predators and singled out in an attempt to lure them.

I have another question for you. Do you know when the highest rate of child sex trafficking occurs in the United States each year? The answer may surprise you as the event is looked upon almost as a national holiday of sorts: the Super Bowl, where friends and families come together each year for a party. Yet, former Texas Attorney General, now Texas Governor Greg Abbott has called this icon of American sporting events the "single largest human trafficking incident in the United States," and humanitarian Cindy McCain, wife of Arizona senator and former presidential candidate John McCain, has called it the "largest human-trafficking venue on the planet." During the weeks leading up to the Super Bowl, there is as much as a 300 percent increase in Internet ads regarding sex trafficking. As a big sports fan, this news greatly troubled me when I first heard it, so much so that I did not watch the game this year. In 2014, 45 pimps were arrested, and 16 children between the ages of 13–17 were rescued by police from the clutches of those who were exploiting and enslaving these children for sexual purposes to those who were attending the Super Bowl (DeGarmo, July 2015-A Foster Parent's Look at Human Trafficking, *Foster Focus Magazine*).

Foster children can be particularly vulnerable to sexual predators. Foster children often experience higher levels of anxiety than other children, and this anxiety can manifest itself in a number of ways. Perhaps the one anxiety that foster children face the most is separation anxiety, which is when a child has excessive anxiety concerning the separation from their home, family, and those to whom they are attached the most. The more a child moves from home to home, from foster placement to foster placement, the bigger the concern becomes. Those children who undergo many displacements often create walls to separate themselves in an attempt not to let others into their lives. (DeGarmo, 2014-Keeping Foster Children Safe Online, JKP). Still others feel starved for a sense of family and belonging. This type of anxiety and insecurity can make them vulnerable to sexual predators as children in foster care search for love. Those foster children who have been abused in some way in the past may be more likely to show inappropriate sexual behavior or seek out love in inappropriate places. Consequently, they may seek out sexual content and relationships through online means.

Sadly, the search for love for many children in foster care leads to a road of sexual exploitation. Foster children often are in need of love yet do not know what a healthy and loving relationship is. What many foster parents do not know, though, is how easy it is for foster children to encounter sexual predators online. These sexual predators know that foster children are particularly vulnerable to this kind of assault (DeGarmo, 2014-Keeping Foster Children Safe Online, JKP). There are specific ways that sexual predators can identify foster children who are online and are using social media sites.

Most prostituted youth today come from environments where they have run away from home and therefore may be homeless, have been victimized in a variety of ways, or may have already been sexually abused in the past.

Along with this influence, many of these children who have already been exposed to sexual abuse have problems with low self-esteem and do not receive the educational opportunities they deserve. To me, these characteristics sound like our foster children, don't you think? Foster children often come from environments with these forms of abuse. Teens that age out of the foster care system are also more likely to end up homeless and may choose a lifestyle of prostitution in order to "make ends meet" financially. These young adults are more inclined to be placed into foster homes or group homes, and are also more likely to run away. Pimps also attract foster children by targeting them in group homes and promising them gifts, a sense of belonging, and a place where they will be loved, all while grooming them for a life as a child prostitute.

The warning in Scripture is pretty strong and undeniable. Those who hurt innocent children and lure them into a den of danger and abuse will face judgment from God, as Jesus said in Luke 17:2:

> IT WOULD BE BETTER FOR HIM IF A MILLSTONE WERE HUNG
> AROUND HIS NECK AND HE WERE CAST INTO THE SEA THAN THAT
> HE SHOULD CAUSE ONE OF THESE LITTLE ONES TO SIN. *(ESV)*

As foster parents and Christians, we are given the charge of protecting these children in need. Without a doubt, so many of these children have experienced situations and terrors that we might not be prepared to address. So many children in foster care have been exposed to environments and horrors that are beyond our own experiences. Yet these are the very children who need to be protected and kept safe from these situations and horrors, ensuring that they never experience them again. God is calling you to protect these children, and He has given you the skills, talents, abilities, and the love to do so. May we all work hard to defend the very least of these.

Praying for Our Children In Foster Care

Prayer is a powerful tool.

God has given us the gift of prayer as a means to communicate with Him, to talk with God. Prayer can strengthen our faith and change our lives as we open ourselves to hear God's Word. As we open ourselves completely to God, laying our concerns and desires before Him, we lean upon Him completely and we reach deep into ourselves, hiding nothing from God as we admit our personal failures. Furthermore, prayer can bring us peace during turbulent times. For me and my wife, prayer allows us to seek God's wisdom and strength each time we get a call from a case worker about taking a foster child into our home. When we pray according to God's will, we are opening up a power that is unstoppable. Jesus told us so Himself when He said, "If you abide in me, and my words abide in you, ask whatever you wish, and it will be done for you" (John 15:7 ESV).

When those who are not foster parents hear that my wife and I usually have an average of eight children in our house at a time, I am often met with the same statement over and over again: "I don't know how you do it." My response is usually, "With a great deal of prayer." Without a doubt, prayer is an important part of fostering. As foster parents, we lean upon God for strength to help these children battle the many emotional, physical, and psychological challenges they face. Along with this strength, we pray we are able to love these children with the unconditional love they so dearly need. I have spoken to numerous foster parents who have spent sleepless nights and worried days lifting up their foster children in prayer during difficult times of visitations with unstable biological parents, court appearances, or when a child leaves their home for another. As a foster parent, I rely upon God on a daily basis, both leaning on Him for strength and asking Him to bless the children with His mercy.

If you read my book *Fostering Love: One Foster Parent's Journey* or the sequel, *Love and Mayhem: One Big Family's Uplifting Story of Fostering and Adoption*, you know then of my daily prayer to find and perhaps rescue our former foster child, Sydney. Sydney lived with us for a year and a half, coming to us when she was seven years old. Sydney grew up in an environment where she basically took care of herself. Living with her severely alcoholic grandmother, this poor, hungry, and neglected child had to find and prepare her own food each morning and evening, which usually consisted of frozen hot dogs warmed in the microwave. She was also responsible for getting herself ready for school each day. As a result, she often missed catching the bus in the morning and had a large amount of absences, resulting in severely poor academic performance. Gone for long periods of time, Sydney's drug-addicted mother would pop in and out of her life. Sydney's father was a registered sex offender. When the seven year old arrived in our home, she was so behind in her school work that she could not even write her own name. Her behavior in school was also very difficult, and I often had to leave work to meet with Sydney and the school principal.

I need to be honest with you. The year and a half with Sydney was challenging and frustrating at times. Despite this difficulty, she became a valued member of our family, and we loved her like a daughter. So it came as quite a shock when we received a call on December 22, a year and a half after she came to live with us. Her caseworker informed us that Sydney would be leaving the next day, giving us less than 24 hours to not only pack her belongings but to say good-bye to our daughter from foster care. Oh, sure, I did argue with the caseworker for Sydney to stay a little longer and be with the only family that the child had truly ever known on Christmas Day. After all, I felt she needed to be surrounded by those who loved her best and had become her family while opening up her bounty of presents on Christmas Day. Despite this plea, two days before Christmas, Sydney left our home and family and moved to Florida as her aunt and uncle had adopted her. I had great reservations and concern regarding this adoption, as she had only met the couple one time. It was a time of much sadness and tears in our home as we all grieved the loss of this special child.

For years, we heard nothing from Sydney, though we prayed for her frequently. My prayer was that Sydney was well, that she was safe, and that her future spouse would be one who was raised in a Christian home, with Christian values and morals, a prayer that I lift up to God each morning for all the children in my home. Four years after Sydney had moved from our home, we received a phone call from her one evening. Picking up the phone that evening, I was met with a familiar voice asking, "Is that you, Daddy?" Instantly recognizing her voice, I was thrilled to speak with her, and both Kelly and I were overjoyed to finally make contact with her. She had been placed into yet another foster home, this time in Alabama, after being bounced from home to home for two years. Sydney had been taken from her aunt and uncle, who heavily abused her, and placed into several different homes over the next several years. Speaking to her foster mother at the time of the call, Kelly discovered that Sydney ran away from her foster home on occasion, had been in trouble a considerable amount, and had simply become difficult to live with. Both my wife and I were stunned that Sydney had called us and had referred to us as the only "Mommy" and "Daddy" in her life. As we were traveling to Australia the next day for three weeks to visit Kelly's mother, we informed Sydney's foster mother that we would call her back when we returned.

Sadly, when we arrived back in the United States, Sydney had already been moved to a group home for foster children, a modern day orphanage of sorts. The foster mother who had only weeks before taken Sydney into her home told Kelly upon our return that the now teenage girl had become so disruptive and undisciplined that she was almost unadoptable. As she did not know the name or location of the group home in which our former daughter of 20 months had been placed, we were unable to locate her. Despite attempts over and over again by both myself and Kelly to locate Sydney, through searches on the Internet, phone calls to various child welfare agencies in Alabama, and though our own connections here in Georgia, we met with failure after failure. To be sure, she would probably cause us a great deal of difficulties, but we felt strongly that we needed to contact her, to let her know that we thought of her, that she was loved, she mattered, and that she was still part of our family. Yet Sydney was once again lost to us, leaving Kelly and I in grief once more.

Five years have passed, and the phone call still haunts me. I often wake up from the same recurring dream, a dream of Sydney lost in the woods or some other location. She is calling my name over and over again. I pray for her each morning as I lift up my prayers for my own children. Along with this prayer, each Sunday evening I spend a half hour trying to locate her through online means. Using various names and information, I search for her through Facebook and other social media sites, through online searches, and through hundreds of emails to numerous child welfare agencies in Georgia, Florida, and Alabama. As she has lived in all of these states, I am unsure where she might be now. Sadly, I have yet to find her. When I do, I am quite certain that she will be difficult, and maybe even too much for us to handle. Yet, I want her to know that she is important, that she is cared for, and that she is loved.

> *Five years have passed, and the phone call still haunts me. I often wake up from the same recurring dream, a dream of Sydney lost in the woods or some other location. She is calling my name over and over again. I pray for her each morning as I lift up my prayers for my own children.*

THE QUESTION OF PRAYER

Perhaps the best way we as foster parents can help our children in foster care is by taking a knee and lifting up our children and our concerns to God through prayer. Many of these children have never had someone pray for them. In fact, they may not even be aware what prayer is.

Helena's Romanian parents were killed when she was nine, and a family in New York adopted her and told her that they would teach her English, be her family, and love her unconditionally. After six months of sexual abuse, they un-adopted her and gave her back to the state's child welfare system. Then, a family from Pennsylvania adopted her, telling her that they would teach her English, be her family, protect her from harm, and love her unconditionally. After one year, they un-adopted her. At age 11, a family from Georgia adopted her and told her that they would finish teaching her English, protect her, and love her unconditionally. You guessed it. After six years of living with them, they placed her into the child welfare system. Then, this 17 year old, who was in so much emotional pain, came to live with us. As you can imagine, she came to us with a tremendous amount of distrust. Why should she trust us after three adoptive families had abandoned her? When Kelly and I spoke to her about unconditional love, she would often question us about it, telling us that she did not believe in it.

Helena was enrolled in the school where I was working during that time. As we were walking out to the car one afternoon, she asked me if she could go out on a date with a teenage boy from another school. I told her that I would discuss it with Kelly and that the two of us would pray about it.

"Do you pray about everything?" I could hear the level of disdain dripping in her voice.

"We surely do," I replied to her, with a smile on my face.

"Why?" she asked.

I was a little taken aback by both her question and her attitude. She was clearly upset. Whether it was because I did not say yes to the potential date with the young man or because Kelly and I were going to pray about it, I was not certain. "Well, Helena," I began, "Miss Kelly and I look to God for all of our decisions, and we look for wisdom from God. It helps our marriage, and it helps us make better decisions."

"I think that's crazy," she responded.

For Helena, prayer was a new concept, and one that she simply did not understand. The Romanian teenager had only known betrayal, pain, and mistrust since her biological parents were taken from her. Like her, so many children enter into care never having experienced the power of prayer or even know who Jesus Christ is. Like me, I am sure you have answered questions from your foster children about who Jesus is, why you go to church, and maybe something as simple as why you pray at the dinner table or at the end of the day. As a foster parent, these are important questions for you to answer and need to be addressed with compassion, understanding, and, of course, prayer. At the same time, it is also very important that you respect any religious differences your foster child has. Allow your foster child to practice his own religious beliefs, and honor those differences and beliefs as well. After all, it is possible that your foster child's birth parents will not want you to take their child to church with you. This situation can be quite difficult for you. Simply because a child is placed in your home does not give you permission to force your religion upon a child or to ignore their own. If you have questions in this regard, contact your child's caseworker and discuss your concerns with him or her.

PRAYER AND THE FOSTER PARENT

There are a number of ways we can pray for our foster children. We need to become prayer warriors for our foster children, lifting them up in prayer on a daily basis. Not only should we pray for the children, but our foster children's caseworkers also need prayer. After all, their job is a difficult one, and they have emotional ties to the children as well. Just today I spoke with a caseworker who told me she worked with a child for over two years who was placed back into a birth parent's home despite the caseworker's pleas. With tears forming in her eyes, this caseworker told me that the concerns she had about the child's reunification with the parents came true, and that she continues to pray for the child each day.

Furthermore, the birth parents of the children are also in need of prayer. Despite the abuse, neglect, and other challenges and horrors the biological parents and birth family members may have placed upon these children, they are children of God, just as you and I are. This calling might be difficult, though. Are we praying for the well-being and healing of the birth parent or for the family to spend more time in jail? Are we praying that the children be reunified with their biological family or that the parent's rights to the child are terminated so we can adopt the child? You may be the only one praying for these parents. We need to put aside our personal judgment and beliefs and instead pray that God's healing hand would move and His will be done for all involved. As Christians, we are called to pray for mercy and justice, not just for the children but for their parents, too. These parents may be victims of abuse, neglect, rape, and violence also. To be honest with you, I remind myself sometimes that I need to walk humbly with our God, that I am a sinner just like anyone else, and that I am no better than those who would hurt their child, my foster child. We all need to keep the words of Micah 6:8 in our hearts when we pray for our foster child's family members. The words of this Scripture verse are both beautiful and powerful reminders of this directive:

> HE HAS SHOWN YOU, O MORTAL, WHAT IS GOOD. AND WHAT DOES THE LORD REQUIRE OF YOU? TO ACT JUSTLY AND TO LOVE MERCY AND TO WALK HUMBLY WITH YOUR GOD.

As a foster parent, there are a number of ways we can pray for our foster children, caseworkers, and biological parents. Let's take some time to look at these important points of prayer:

1. We can pray for the children who are coming into foster care right at this very moment. Pray that these children in need are placed with loving, supportive foster families who are able to meet each child's specific needs. Pray for these children in need as they face the emotionally confusing and traumatic experience of being taken from their family members and being placed into a new home.

2. We can pray that children in foster care do not experience multiple disruptions or move from foster home to foster home to foster home. Each time a child is moved from one home to another, it is a time of trauma and loss. The lack of stability in a home environment is incredibly difficult and challenging on so many levels. Pray that the child is placed in a home that will provide the structure, stability, resources, and love that he so dearly needs, and that he remain in this home until he is able to reunify with his parents, find an adoptive family, or be placed into his forever home.

3. We can pray that the children remain in foster care for as short a time as is safely possible. The more time a child remains in care, the more likely it is that he will not find his forever home and a loving family that will care for him. Pray that God

prepares the hearts and home of a loving forever family if his parental rights are terminated.

4. We can pray that the child is able to form a healthy relationship with his caseworker and that the caseworker is loving, kind, compassionate, and understanding to his needs.

5. We can pray that if the child has siblings in other foster homes, they are all able to stay in contact with each other. Pray that, if it possible and healthy, the siblings are able to remain in a foster home together.

6. We can pray that God heals the trauma, pain, and profound damage to which these children have been exposed. Pray that God will also protect them from any other dangers or threats that they might face in their lives.

7. We can pray that the judge, caseworkers, and those who decide the child's fate receive the wisdom they need in order to make the best decision that is in the child's best interest. If parental rights should be terminated, pray this action is done as painlessly as possible for all involved.

8. We can pray for teens that have aged out of the foster care system. Pray that they do not experience the dangers and horrors that often await them, like homelessness, incarceration, drug usage, prostitution, unemployment, and other threats. Pray that they find a loving Christian family that will look after them, care for them, and mentor them, in both good times and bad. Pray that they find Jesus Christ as their Savior and develop a personal relationship with Him.

9. We can pray that we as foster parents can be the hands, feet, voice, and heart of our loving God. Pray that we are able to share with these children in our care the fruit of the Spirit that God has blessed each of us with.

10. We can pray for the biological children of our foster parents, that they are instruments of God's love, and that their hearts are open to their foster sibling.

11. We can pray that more people would choose to follow the

path of becoming foster parents. With hundreds of thousands of children in foster care and so few foster parents, the need is strong, yet so few are willing to pick up this cross of service.

12. We can pray for the birth parents and biological family members. Pray that they find the strength they need to overcome their personal demons, such as drug and alcohol addiction, incarceration, unemployment, mental illness, or other challenges they face. Pray that they receive the resources, programs, and help they need. Pray that they are able to make a full and complete recovery so that they can be loving parents, allowing for a safe and healthy reunification with their children. Pray that they also come to know Christ as their Savior.

13. We can pray for the social workers. Pray that they find wisdom to place a child into the right home, a home that is best suited for both the child and the family. Pray that they receive the strength they need with the many difficult aspects of their jobs. Pray that they receive the compassion and love they need to share with both the children and their biological family members.

14. We can pray that social workers receive the funding and resources they need from the state. Pray that they also find joy and satisfaction in their job and that they rely upon God.

15. We can pray that the lawmakers in each state make decisions that are best for the children as well as for the foster parents. Pray that these lawmakers and politicians have their eyes and hearts open to the realities that children in foster care face, as well as the challenges and frustrations that foster parents and caseworkers face. Pray that our lawmakers turn to God for His wisdom in these decisions.

16. We can pray that our churches hear the call to help children in foster care, and that they answer this call from God with grace and mercy. Pray that our churches and church leaders are equipped with the resources and support that is needed for this missions field and that they make an immediate impact in the lives of foster children, and in foster care in general.

Cybil's Story

Years ago, we had a little girl in our care, and she knew nothing of God. When she first arrived, she did not understand why we prayed before each meal, so I sat her down and told her about who God is and how He lives in each of us, takes care of us, and, most of all, loves us. She liked that idea. I also told her that He sees her every day, and even though she couldn't see Him, He was there. Then came the time when she had been with us about five days and it was Sunday morning. We went to church, and she was impressed with how big that place was but still had no idea of why we were there. I sat down and started making out a check for offering (tithing). She asked what I was doing, so I proceeded to tell her, "Remember how we pray before each meal and give thanks that God provided this food for us?" She responded with a nod yes, and I went on to tell her that I was writing a check because we were in God's house that morning, and this check was for Him. She got all excited and very loudly said, "It's about time; I gotta see Him!" All the little elderly ladies around me started giggling because it was cute. Just then the choir started coming out of the choir loft to take their seats, and they had on their robes. She loudly said, "I bet He is going to follow those angels in." It was priceless.

She went on to learn more about God before leaving my home and knew that God was with her even when she left my home, and that made her feel good inside, she said.

YOUR MARRIAGE: PARTNERING WITH GOD AS YOU CARE FOR HIS CHILDREN

"Let me pray about this decision with my wife, and I will call you back," I said to the caseworker before saying good-bye to her. It was just past dinnertime, and we had received a call to take three children into our home. For some time, Kelly had been telling me that she was tired and did not want to foster anymore due to her heart being broken over and over. To be sure, we needed to pray about this decision.

"That was Lisa, the caseworker, on the phone. She wants to know if we can take a group of three siblings into our home," I told her with a nervous smile on my face. I was unsure what to expect from my wife, and I was not so sure that I was prepared to have nine children under our roof by the end of the night.

"How old are they?" she asked with a small sigh escaping her lips.

"There is a ten-year-old boy, an 11-year-old girl, and a 13-year-old boy," I replied. With the information I received from Lisa, I then told Kelly what I knew about the children. The three came from a home that had no electricity, water, food, or plumbing. The parents were on drugs, and there were drugs in the house. Moving from home to home and from city to city, the children were seldom in school. Violence, sexual abuse, and psychological issues were just some of the challenges the children faced. The youngest boy was full of anger, the sister was passive aggressive, and the oldest was the worst behaved student in his school. Yet these were all children of God, and all needed a home this night.

Standing in the middle of the kitchen, I took Kelly's hand in mine. "Let's pray," I said to her. "Heavenly Father, we thank You for the many blessings You have given us. Thank You, Lord, for the healthy children we have in our home, and for bringing so many children into our home to love. Lord, we thank You for the opportunity to serve You and to help those who are in need. Yet, Lord, You know that we are a little tired and have so much already on our plate. We just don't know if we can do it. Give us insight, Lord, on what You would have us do. We know that with You, all things are possible. Open our hearts, please, so we can know what decision we should make. Help us to see clearly if we should take these children who are hurting and who are scared into our home. If it is Your will, give us the strength and wisdom to care for them. If we are unable to do it, please find a loving Christian home for these children, Lord. It is in Your name that we pray. Amen."

Looking at my wife, I let out a deep sigh and asked Kelly the all too familiar question, one that I had asked her several times during the years in situations just like tonight: "Well, what do you think?"

"These children need us," my wife answered with sadness echoing in both her voice and in her eyes. "I think you should call Lisa back and tell her we will take them." Squeezing my hand, she gave me a reassuring smile.

Without a doubt, I would never be able to be a good foster parent if it were not for my wife. She brings so many strengths to our parenting, whether it is with our own children or our foster children. My wife complements me in so many areas, as I do to her. We both rely on each other to be parents to so many children who have passed through our home. After all, marriage is a gift from God, and Scripture points to this fact several times. Let us take a look at some of these verses and what the Bible says about marriage:

THEN THE LORD GOD MADE A WOMAN FROM THE RIB HE HAD TAKEN OUT OF THE MAN, AND HE BROUGHT HER TO THE MAN. THE MAN SAID, "THIS IS NOW BONE OF MY BONES AND FLESH OF MY FLESH; SHE SHALL BE CALLED 'WOMAN,' FOR SHE WAS TAKEN OUT OF MAN." THAT IS WHY A MAN LEAVES HIS FATHER AND MOTHER AND IS UNITED TO HIS WIFE, AND THEY BECOME ONE FLESH. —GENESIS 2:22–24

He who finds a wife finds what is good and receives favor from the LORD. —Proverbs 18:22

A wife of noble character who can find? She is worth far more than rubies. —Proverbs 31:10

"Haven't you read," he replied, "that at the beginning the Creator 'made them male and female,' and said, 'For this reason a man will leave his father and mother and be united to his wife, and the two will become one flesh'? So they are no longer two, but one flesh. Therefore what God has joined together, let no one separate." —Matthew 19:4–6

Before Kelly and I became foster parents many years ago, we both did a great deal of research into what it meant, the responsibilities involved, and how it would affect both our family and our marriage. We spoke to other foster parents, did plenty of reading on the subject, discussed it with each other, and prayed about it daily. What we saw, read, and heard was something that we both felt was right for us and felt called to do. Yet perhaps the most important component of all of this process was that we were both in agreement on it and unified in this decision. After all, fostering can be exhausting at times, stressful some days, and even bring sadness to our family when children leave our homes. Foster parenting must be a joint and unified decision by both partners in a marriage, without doubt from either person, as it will take a 100 percent effort from both of you. Both you and your spouse must be fully committed emotionally, physically, and mentally to the many responsibilities of taking care of children in need, as it will require all of those traits. If one person is not committed to being a foster parent, then the foster child will suffer, your family will suffer, and your marriage will suffer as well.

Foster Care and Parenting Challenges

Being a foster parent can be both rewarding and exhausting. There are days when the joys and successes can be rewarding and exhilarating. There are also those days when the disappointments and frustrations can be challenging. To be sure, these disappointments and frustrations as a foster parent can be difficult and even damaging to a marriage. Here are some ways that your marriage can be hurt while being a foster parent:

YOUR MARRIAGE CAN BE NEGLECTED. Being a foster parent takes tremendous time and energy. When you are looking after a child from foster care 24 hours a day, every day, every week, every month, it can be time consuming and leave little time for you and your spouse. My wife and I have not had a date night in almost two years, I am afraid to say. Before we were foster parents, we tried to go out once a month, just the two of us. Now, we have to retreat to our bedroom with doors closed just to find time and privacy for even a few words together. With so many children and so many demands from needy ones, it often leaves little time for our marriage.

YOUR OWN NEEDS CAN BE IGNORED. For those foster parents who are extremely busy with children in their home, they may find that they have little time not only for their marriage but for themselves as well. Hobbies, interests, personal space, friendships, and simple time alone often disappear altogether when being a foster parent. This loss can place added stress upon a marriage.

THE CONSTRAINT OF FINANCES. Despite what some might say, you are certainly not fostering for the money. As you and I both know, it can be financially stressful when taking care of foster children. There are those times when the needs of our children from foster care can be rather expensive, causing further strain on our financial well-being.

LACK OF SLEEP. It was my night on duty last night, and I was up four times between 11 p.m. and 6 a.m. caring for our latest foster son who was born ten weeks premature. Are we getting much sleep in our house at the moment? Not a chance in the world, my friend. My wife and I have to be careful not to let the lack of sleep affect our moods. Our lack of sleep could certainly hurt our marriage and our relationships with others.

A DISAGREEMENT ON DISCIPLINE. When there are disagreements on how to discipline a child in your home, it can cause a serious strain on a marriage. One parent may see a form of punishment or consequences as not severe enough, while another may see it as too strict.

WORKING WITH BIOLOGICAL PARENTS. During my years as a foster parent, I have been cursed, had objects thrown at me, spat upon, and lied about in court. My wife has even been followed in a car on two separate occasions. In the eyes of some biological parents, foster parents are the bad guys, the ones who took their children away. Foster parents represent a part of their lives that they may not want to remember or even refuse to acknowledge. There are those times when working with biological parents can be stressful for all involved.

THE NEEDS OF THE CHILDREN MAY BE EXHAUST-ING. You may have foster children placed in your home who are emotionally needy, physically sick, sexually abused, or mentally ill. Along with these challenges, there may be behavioral issues as well. Make no mistake, these illnesses and conditions can be strenuous and very tiring to a parent, thus causing further stress and anxiety upon a marriage.

DISAGREEMENTS BETWEEN MARRIED COUPLES. In all marriages, like any partnership, there are bound to be disagreements. Whether it is about the discipline of a child, financial situations, child rearing, work related issues, or even about the in-laws, you will not agree with your spouse on everything. Sometimes, disagreements may lead to arguments between you and your spouse, bringing even further stress to your marriage.

CHILDREN MANIPULATING ONE AGAINST THE OTHER. Some foster children have the ability to use manipulation in their favor as they pit one foster parent against the other. They might say something like, "My foster dad said he would let me play those video games; why won't you?" or "Why can't I go? My foster mom said I could go out to see that movie. It's not fair that you won't let me go." When this type of manipulation occurs, it brings a level of division to your marriage, causing tension between the two of you.

RESENTMENT OF THE CHILD IN YOUR HOME. It always disturbs me to hear from a foster parent who says that his or her spouse resents having a foster child in the house living with them. A few months ago, I listened as a foster father told me about how he and his wife were at odds about the teenage foster son in their home. It seems that the troubled teenager was constantly in trouble at both school and home and was most defiant toward the foster father. His wife did not want to "give up" on the child, while the husband felt that their foster son needed to be placed in another home. As a result, their marriage was under duress as the two were at disagreement on him being placed in their home, and resentment was building in the husband toward the child.

SAYING GOOD-BYE TO A CHILD. Whenever a child leaves your home, there are bound to be feelings of loss and grief of some sort. After all, you have not only come to protect and provide for this child, but you have also come to love him like your own, and he has become a member of your family. You might also experience feelings of guilt if you asked for a foster child to be removed from your home. These feelings of grief, loss, or guilt can lead to depression. When foster parents experience such feelings, it can bring an added stress and burden to a marriage.

Monica and Anthony's Story

My husband and I had been struggling with the fact that our foster daughter was having problems adjusting to our home. The nine-year-old girl had been with us for seven months and still had not allowed herself to open her heart to us. Maybe because she had already been in four different foster homes over the course of a year and a half before she came to live with us. Maybe it was because her own mother and father would beat her. Maybe it was because she simply didn't trust us or know how to trust us.

We tried a number of ways to break down the walls that she placed around her. All my husband and I wanted to do was to hug her, tell her that we loved her, and that she was going to be safe. Every time we tried to do this, though, she would push us away with both her hands and her words, yelling at us and running to her room before slamming the door. Many nights, I would hear her crying while I cried also. My heart just broke for her, as I knew she was hurting desperately inside.

After a while, it wasn't just pushing away and saying mean things to us like she did the first five months. She began to throw things at my husband and I, and her behavior in school was getting worse, too. Our little girl was coming home with reports from her teacher that she was also saying mean-spirited and hateful words to the other students in her class as well as the teacher. On two occasions, I had to meet with her and the teacher to discuss her attitude, but it didn't seem to change the situation.

FOSTER PARENTING AND MARRIED LIFE

As we can see, there are many obstacles that can challenge a healthy marriage when becoming a foster parent. To be sure, being a foster parent will change your life in so many ways. Therefore, it will be absolutely necessary that you take steps to protect your marriage from any of the slings and arrows that might threaten your foster parenting and your marriage.

BE UNITED AS A FAMILY. As we saw earlier, it is most important that you and your spouse are both in agreement when it comes to being a foster parent. There will be times when you will rely upon your spouse for help, strength, and to make decisions. Furthermore, if you have children of your own living with you, you will also need them to be supportive and on board with your decision to care for foster children. Your own children may have concerns. Perhaps they are worried that they will have to share you with their new foster sibling. They may resent that there is a new person joining their family. Ask them to share their feelings with you, and listen to what they have to say. Reassure your own children that you will always be there for them. You will also want to plan on setting aside some special time for just you and your own children, as they will need time alone with you during your fostering.

TAKE TIME FOR YOUR MARRIAGE. Our marriage is a gift from our Heavenly Father, a gift that we do not want to have taken from us. Sadly, I have known foster couples whose marriages have fallen apart due to the stresses they encountered while taking care of children in need. Other couples to whom I have spoken tell me that they spend so much time caring for the children in their home that they leave little time for themselves. Every marriage needs both partners to put work into it in order for the marriage to be a healthy one. Therefore, it is necessary that you spend some alone time with your spouse as often as possible. Perhaps schedule a date night once every two weeks or once a month. If you are like my wife and me, and scheduled date nights are simply not possible, perhaps plan a lunch together, a walk in the neighborhood, or another activity that allows the two of you to have some private time together. This time alone is important, as you can share your concerns, desires, hopes, and wants, not only as a foster parent but as a married couple. Another way to spend time together is by closing the bedroom door once a week, grabbing some snacks and food, and watching a movie in bed together. Waking up early in the morning for some prayer time together is another great way to stay connected with your spouse. This practice also allows you the important opportunity to bring both of your concerns and joys to God, united together in prayer. However you do it, it is vital to your marriage and to your well-being that you find time for you and your spouse. Work to make your marriage the cornerstone of your home, and work to make it a productive and happy one.

TAKE TIME FOR YOURSELF. I know of some people that become so engrossed in being a parent and taking care of children that their own personal identity disappears over time. Now, being a parent is a wonderful calling and a gift from God. Yet you as a person, as an individual, are just as much a gift from God. Don't neglect who you are and what makes you special. After all, your spouse fell in love with you for who you are! Try to engage in your hobbies and interests as often as you can. Go out to lunch with friends. Read some books for enjoyment or for self-help. Don't forget some personal quiet time as well. For me, I often find this time as I drive to and from work. I am amazed how lovely silence sounds when I turn off the radio and allow my thoughts to wander. I also use this time for prayers. If you keep yourself happy and in a good mood, it will help to ensure that you are in a better mood for your foster child, your spouse, and others.

KEEP COMMUNICATION ESSENTIAL. Any good marriage is built on strong communication. In fact, many experts say it is the most important tool you can use for your marriage. Be open and honest about your feelings with your spouse, and do not hide things from your partner. If something is bothering you, share this concern with your loved one. When your spouse shares their concerns with you, be sure to listen; simply listen. I want to be able to fix my wife's problem as soon as she tells me. I have learned that this approach is not always what she wants or needs. Instead, she simply wants me to listen to her.

REMOVE DISTRACTIONS. When you are having an open and honest conversation with your spouse, make sure there are no distractions around. Turn off the TV, radio, computer, and phone. Try to find some place where you will be uninterrupted by children, perhaps behind locked doors in your bedroom. In my home, we have had plenty of little foster children simply walk in our room unannounced. Also, ensure that you are giving your spouse eye contact during the conversation. Make sure that you never ridicule or become defensive about what your spouse has to say. Instead, remain patient and compassionate, even if the conversation is a difficult one. Furthermore, try to make sure that you are more positive than negative in your comments. As noted earlier, try to create alone time as often as you can with your spouse, as this privacy will help greatly in your communication.

WORK TOGETHER TO BE IN AGREEMENT. I was pleasantly surprised just a few weeks ago when my 14-year-old foster son said to my wife and me, "You two are the nicest people I have ever met. You never raise your voice at each other and never argue." Despite the fact that he had been living with us for over a year, he was incorrect on one thing; my wife and I do argue on occasion. It's normal for married couples to argue once in a while. When we do, we make sure that it is never in front of the children and that our disagreements are not mean-spirited or offensive. Furthermore, we both try to make sure that our arguments are relevant to the conversation and to the issue at hand and that they are temporary. When it comes to issues of child rearing, discipline, and other issues that relate to our foster parenting, it is necessary that you and your spouse try to be in agreement with these issues. Be willing to be flexible and to overlook small and minor disagreements.

BE UNITED WITH YOUR SPOUSE. Do not let the children's behavior separate the two of you. As we noted earlier, there are those children who will test you and your relationship with your spouse. Some foster children, like all children, know how to manipulate one parent over the other. Remain united with your spouse, and make sure that you do not allow a foster child to come between you. Along with this commitment, do not take your foster child's behaviors personally. Keep in mind that his behavior is a learned one, probably from the previous environment from which he came. Your foster child is behaving the way he was taught and allowed to act before he came to live with you. Do not let his behaviors affect you and your marriage.

USE RESOURCES AND FIND HELP. If you are like me, you like the process of learning new things. I truly enjoy learning as much as possible about a topic in which I am interested and seek out resources and information to help me better understand something about which I want to know more. We all do so with our personal interests and hobbies as it makes us knowledgeable and proficient at something we enjoy. For foster parents, there is an explosion of information being released, each day it seems, related to foster care. New books, websites, articles, and other resources are becoming available on a larger scale than ever before. When you seek out and locate help and resources about all things foster care, you become a stronger foster parent and thus help to strengthen your marriage as well.

FIND SUPPORT IN A GROUP. Perhaps the best thing I did after going through my initial training as a foster parent was to join my local foster parent association. This group of foster parents, all living in my area, comes together each month for a number of reasons. To begin, we have training each month in order to keep our requirement training hours up to date in our state. Along with this training, we offer each other support and resources, sharing with each other our wisdom from previous experiences as well as providing a listening ear. Finally, I believe the reason I enjoy the meetings the most is the fellowship that is offered. No one really understands a foster parent like another foster parent. We can laugh and cry at each other's stories as well as look for guidance from people who have experienced similar situations.

SEEK HELP FROM STATE AND NATIONAL ORGANIZATIONS. Not only can you find support from a local foster parent association, there are also great state led organizations. Along with these resources, the National Foster Parent Association is a wonderful nationwide support group of foster parents that brings foster parents and advocates together from across the country. There are also faith-based groups and organizations that support foster children and parents. You might find that your church, or another church in your area, is hearing God's call to help foster children and parents. As I travel across the nation, I continue to encounter some amazing churches that are working with foster care as a form of outreach mission. A supportive group for your journey and work as a foster parent will help to relieve some of the stresses that threaten to overcome your marriage.

LEARN TO SAY NO. OK, I must admit to you, this discipline is one that my wife and I are not so good at doing. As you know by now, my wife has said that she was through being a foster parent on several occasions due to years of a broken heart for the children. Yet each time the phone rings and there is a child in need, she always says, "Yes," despite her earlier directives to me. Both Kelly and I try to live out the life of a servant of God in all that we do. Perhaps that is why we recently had 11 children in our home, and perhaps this service might be one reason why we were quite exhausted during that period of our life. Goodness, even parenting nine children was rather tiring at times with the myriad emotional challenges with which many of the children wrestled.

There are times in all of our lives when our plates are full and our limit has been reached. Sometimes, we say yes to too many requests and take on more than we can handle. When this overload occurs, stress builds, responsibilities are not met, and we cease to be helpful. Instead, we become even more exhausted and overburdened and may experience feelings of depression. Without a doubt, your marriage will be harmed as well. No is a powerful word, and as servants of God, it can be a difficult word to say to others who are seeking our help. Yet there are times when we all need to say it. Therefore, we need to make sure that we do not overextend ourselves. After all, God does not want us to go beyond His will.

TAKE THE OPPORTUNITY FOR RESPITE CARE. As I mentioned in *The Foster Parenting Manual*, "There are those times when foster parents will require a short-term break from a foster child. This break may be the result of foster parents traveling on vacation, a temporary move into a new home, or it may be that the birth children in the foster home require some much-needed time with their own parents. Along with this, respite may be used simply because some foster parents are trying to prevent burnout and need a break from their foster child. Other foster parents are often used for respite, as they are officially licensed to look after foster children, and will be reimbursed for the interim that the foster child is placed in their home." If your marriage is under duress and you feel like you can't continue much further, you might wish to consider this option.

POWER OF PRAYER IN A MARRIAGE

Remember when I told you about my discussion with Helena when she asked me if Kelly and I always pray about everything? Well, we do, and it is the most important tool we have in our marriage when battling the slings and arrows that threaten our foster parenting and our union together. Marriage is designed by God and is a gift from Him to us. Prayer is the key to keeping a marriage strong. After all, I am sure you have heard the old saying, "the family that prays together stays together." God does want us to pray together as a married couple and longs for us to come to Him united in prayer. The words of Scripture are quite clear when Jesus says:

> *AGAIN, TRULY I TELL YOU THAT IF TWO OF YOU ON EARTH AGREE ABOUT ANYTHING THEY ASK FOR, IT WILL BE DONE FOR THEM BY MY FATHER IN HEAVEN. FOR WHERE TWO OR THREE GATHER IN MY NAME, THERE AM I WITH THEM.* —MATTHEW *18:19–20*

There are a number of ways prayer can benefit both your marriage and your foster parenting. Prayer is a conversation as you share your concerns, desires, struggles, and joys with a loving God who wants to spend time with you and your spouse. When you pray together as a couple, a number of benefits begin to open for your marriage.

PRAYER UNITES YOU AND YOUR SPOUSE SPIRITU-ALLY WITH OUR HEAVENLY FATHER. As you spend time in prayer, your own relationship with your spouse will begin to deepen as the two of you become united together. Your own communication will be strengthened as the two of you bring your concerns and wishes to God.

PRAYER ENCOURAGES A HUMBLE HEART. Prayer is a humbling experience. When you and your spouse bring your concerns and worries to God, relying upon Him, you will find that your own pride and own dependency begin to break down. Indeed, the more you and your spouse rely upon God and make Him the center of your marriage, the stronger your marriage becomes.

PRAYER HELPS THOSE WHO ARE IN NEED. As we noted in the previous chapter, there are a number of ways you can pray for others. We saw that we can pray for our foster children, caseworkers, and biological family members. To be sure, God wants us to lift these people up in prayer, and He does answer our prayers. Sometimes we may see His answers, and other times we may not. Never doubt, though, that God does hear us, that He does answer our prayers. We need to pray for our foster children in particular on a daily basis and do so together, as a married couple. When we pray for our foster children, our own hearts are softened toward these children, and our love for them grows. Quite simply, your foster children need you and your spouse to devote time together praying for them. This prayer might be the greatest gift you can give them.

CHARONNE'S STORY

It has been a heartbreaking couple of months in our home as we have walked through the healing process with one of our little ones. It has left me feeling overwhelmed, feeling like I've done something wrong or not given enough, feeling like we may never see the light at the end of the tunnel, feeling heartbroken.

Our hearts are already broken for children and families who find themselves a part of the child welfare system. That heartbreak is why we chose to foster in the first place.

Our hearts are broken over the abuse and neglect the children who come into our home have experienced.

Our hearts are broken that these children are removed from their family and their home (as unhealthy and unstable as it was) and brought to the arms of a stranger.

Our hearts are broken that we cannot undo or fully understand the pain they have experienced.

Our hearts are broken that this child has siblings out there from whom she's been separated.

Our hearts are broken the first time you see that hurting little girl play and smile so big it lights up her entire face, a smile like no other, which you could never forget.

Our hearts are broken when their parents continue to let them down and fail to show up for them.

Our hearts are broken when their parents get it together and show they are ready to parent their child, and the little one we have loved as our own moves on.

Our hearts are broken when parental rights are terminated, making it possible for our child whom we love with our entire being to become a part of our family forever, all the while grieving this great loss for our child and her family of origin.

Our hearts break that we can't do more.

Our hearts break that our country needs a foster care system.

Our hearts break for all the broken families.

Our hearts break knowing that for a short time or forever we have been given the gift of loving this child.

Loving Your Child's Birth Parents

OK, this chapter might be tough for some. For a long time, it was tough for me. I struggled for my first couple of years as a foster parent with praying for the people who hurt my foster child.

Praying for the birth parents of your foster child is one important area of foster care that we as Christians need to be doing on a regular basis. This responsibility may be the most difficult part of your job. To begin with, these people may have abused or neglected your foster child. Helping them might just be the last thing you wish to do. Praying for them might be even harder. After all, there is a reason why many of these children are in foster care, and this reason has to do with how their birth parents and biological family members treated them. Perhaps mistreated is a better word.

During my third year as a foster parent, I was confronted with this very situation, this very challenge, if you will. Some friends of mine were fostering a six-month-old baby. This tiny little infant, this innocent child of God, this precious miracle of birth, was in a full body cast from his neck down. It still makes me shudder today as I share this story with you almost ten years later. His father had beaten his son against a bedpost several times, breaking many of the tiny baby's bones. Along with these injuries, his body was covered with teeth marks from where his mother would bite down upon her son in her own anger. A mother and father both treating their newborn baby with such acts of horror was unthinkable to me. His parents were blessed by God with a gift to love, a gift that would love them back, and instead they almost killed this tiny, defenseless baby. When my friend first told me about their newest foster baby, I was sickened by such acts of atrocity. Yet what I found out later that night made me full of anger. The baby boy's parents were both teenagers from another county, teenagers in the very school at which I taught, only 45 minutes from where I lived. Even more difficult to hear was that both of the parents were students in classes I was teaching at the time.

When I went to school each day during that time, I did pray. Yet at that time, I prayed selfishly. I prayed for me, not for the baby's parents, my two students. What I wanted to do was take the teenage father and slam him against the school locker, hurting him for what he did to his baby, his son. I wanted to say hurtful things to the baby's mother. I was so angry, so very angry, and simply could not understand how two people could hurt a helpless child. I wanted somehow to make these parents pay for what they did to the baby now in foster care. Instead, I prayed for myself to have the patience to control my own emotions when it came to both the mother and father.

> I wanted somehow to make these parents pay for what they did to the baby now in foster care. Instead, I prayed for myself to have the patience to control my own emotions when it came to both the mother and father.

Years later, I realized that I was mistaken in my prayers. Indeed, I did pray for the baby and for his foster parents, which is one area for which I should have been praying. Yet along with praying for myself, I should have also been praying for my two students, the very two people who had literally almost destroyed the life of this helpless baby. I should have prayed that God would heal them from whatever pain and issues they were going through. I should have prayed that they receive forgiveness for these actions not only from God but also from others, including myself. I should have prayed for ways to reach out to them, to help them, to be a mentor or guide to them. Sadly, I did not realize this need until much later, after the two parents had left my classroom. God had given me a chance to be a blessing to these two, to reach out to them and share God's love and forgiveness with the very ones who had severely abused their only child. Instead, I did not, and I still regret not doing so. Since then, I have asked God several times to forgive me of my own sins of judgment against these two students, these children of God.

Loving those in need, even those who don't deserve it, is exactly what God calls us to do. Like my two former students, those birth parents and biological family members who abuse, abandon, and neglect children in foster care are all children of our loving God. God loves those who hurt children just as much as He loves those who protect children. As foster parents we are fallen, sinful human beings who need God's forgiveness and grace just as much as our foster child's birth parents.

Sometimes, I need a reminder of this truth when I face a child who has suffered horribly, much like the child whose mother burned him with cigarettes, a story I shared with you earlier. Indeed, the Bible warns us many times about not judging others. Here are a few:

Judge not, that you be not judged. For with the judgment you pronounce you will be judged, and with the measure you use it will be measured to you. Why do you see the speck that is in your brother's eye, but do not notice the log that is in your own eye? Or how can you say to your brother, "Let me take the speck out of your eye," when there is the log in your own eye? You hypocrite, first take the log out of your own eye, and then you will see clearly to take the speck out of your brother's eye.
—Matthew 7:1–5 (ESV)

Do not speak evil against one another, brothers. The one who speaks against a brother or judges his brother, speaks evil against the law and judges the law. But if you judge the law, you are not a doer of the law but a judge. There is only one lawgiver and judge, he who is able to save and to destroy. But who are you to judge your neighbor? —James 4:11–12 (ESV)

Therefore you have no excuse, O man, every one of you who judges. For in passing judgment on another you condemn yourself, because you, the judge, practice the very same things. We know that the judgment of God rightly falls on those who practice such things.

Do you suppose, O man—you who judge those who practice such things and yet do them yourself—that you will escape the judgment of God? —Romans 2:1–3 (ESV)

Judge not, and you will not be judged; condemn not, and you will not be condemned; forgive, and you will be forgiven.
—Luke 6:37 (ESV)

We have discussed the importance of unconditional love and how necessary it is for our foster children to receive this kind of love from us. Indeed, we love these children because God loves us first. If we are truly to love God and truly follow His command to love others like our foster children, we are also to love the birth parents with an unconditional love. Maybe you disagree with their parenting styles. Maybe their morals and values differ completely from yours. Maybe they have said mean things against you. We are called to love all of God's children. Even if they have committed unspeakable abuse against the children, we are to love them. Even if they have abandoned the children, we are to love them. Even if they have been rude and mean-spirited against us, we are to love them.

As I shared in *The Foster Parenting Manual*, "Therefore, it is important that you do not prejudge them before you meet them. . . . What is also important to consider, though, is that many biological parents of foster children were abused themselves and know of no other way when raising children. Also disturbing is that some birth parents were foster children as well and are just repeating the cycle they went through as a child. Certainly, there are reasons why their children are in care that we may never understand."

I recently spoke with a foster father who adopted three of his foster children. The children were all under the age of four, with the youngest only six months old. Their mother had been a foster child herself and spent most of her youth being sent from one foster home to another. When she was 12, she was reunified with her birth father, who started exchanging her to others for sex to support his drug habit. By the time she was 16, she had already had an abortion. She aged out of care at 18 and became a prostitute, which she is still today. Now, all three of her children, from three different fathers, are in foster care, continuing a cycle of sadness and tragedy from which the mother never escaped herself. Imagine if she had been loved unconditionally. Imagine if she had been lifted up in prayer each day. I was delighted to hear that the foster father is doing this very thing. He has reached out to the mother of his adopted girls and is praying for her daily.

In chapter 4, we looked at ways to pray for those involved in foster care, including our foster child's birth parents. To be sure, our prayers for our child's birth parents should be a consistent part of our regular prayers. When we pray for people who have hurt our foster children or even have hurt us, we are not only helping them, but we are also helping ourselves. By praying for our child's birth parents, or anyone who is mean-spirited or difficult, we begin to change ourselves as we draw closer to God. This simple act of prayer for our child's biological family helps to deepen our own hearts as it breaks down barriers we may have placed between ourselves and the parents of our foster child. Along with this breaking of barriers, it helps us to forgive those who have wronged our children and ourselves, just as God has forgiven us for our many sins. To be sure, we will grow spiritually in our faith when we pray for all of God's people, including even the most abusive of our foster child's birth parents. As we pray for these birth parents, instead of just praying about them, we just might receive more blessings ourselves as our own hearts are changed.

TAMMY'S STORY

Twelve years ago my husband and I started fostering. Little did we know that our family would grow as a result. We received "the call" to take two little girls ages six and one. It wasn't an easy two-year process. The one year old cried constantly. She didn't want to be held and never liked crowds or loud noises. She was only happy when she was in her bed. She had come from a family where drugs and alcohol were an issue. Visitations, court dates, and lots of prayers took place over the next two years. At the last court date, caseworkers and CASA, or Court Appointed Special Advocate, workers recommended for the children to remain with us. My husband and I are Christians and had prayed for the children to remain with us. God had a different plan, though. The judge ruled for the girls to go back home to their birth mother. We were crushed. The life sucked out of us. Confused and depressed, we were lost without our two little girls.

Our resource developer from the child welfare agency knew just what we needed, another child. We got "the call" to take a five-month-old little girl. We took our baby girl and right from the start, we worked with the baby's birth parents. We kept them informed, sent pictures, and were involved in visits. We even had visits at our home. We felt from the beginning we should be fostering the mom, too. She was young and just wasn't mature enough to have a child. The birth father was from Mexico and quickly saw that his daughter was receiving the best care and love from us. We received a call from the birth father first that he was going to surrender his rights to her. He wanted his daughter raised where she would receive a good education and where there was love in the home. Not long after this call, the birth mother did the same. This all took place over two years.

After the adoption of our baby girl, we still keep in contact with her birth parents. This is an extension of our family. The parents are invited to attend church with us. A couple of times a year we will meet somewhere to eat lunch together. On several occasions, the birth father has spent holidays with us, just as families do.

By the time our baby girl was three years old, we found out our two little girls we had previously fostered were now living with an aunt and uncle. The birth mom was in trouble with drugs yet again. We contacted our child welfare agency and requested to take the children if they needed care. Talk about trusting the Lord and having faith. Three years had passed since they left our home. Not a day had passed when we didn't pray for them. We had no contact with them. All we could do was to have faith that God would take care of them and provide for their needs. I had never felt so helpless. They had been physically abused and had seen a lot of things a child shouldn't see. The girls did come back to live with us, though, and from the start, we bonded with the birth mom this time. It wasn't long after they had been placed with us when the birth mother signed her rights away. We adopted these two, and we are now a family of three girls, and another birth mother is added to our family as well. Through it all, we have relied on our faith. Faith is believing in the unseen and unknown. We have had faith through our fostering. Faith in knowing God is going to provide. Faith that God will give us strength. Faith that God will give us wisdom.

It has now been six years since we adopted these two girls, and over the years we have seen their birth mother on a monthly basis and had weekly phone calls. She has turned her life around and now has two more children. She has told me I am more family to her than her own family has been.

She attends activities that the girls are involved in such as church, soccer, and band. On our last visit to see her, I was given a big surprise. We walked in, and she told the girls she wanted to talk with them. She told them she was sorry she had not been a good mother and she had done a lot of bad things in her life. She wanted them to know what she had done was wrong and that isn't the way they should ever live. She told them they should never take drugs. It was all so very emotional, and we were all crying. We had come full circle. Hopefully our faith and our walk with Christ had shown this birth-mother there is a different way of life. If we had been able to adopt the girls in the beginning, our extended family may never have been able to include the birth mother. All this was a part of God's plan. The process of adopting and fostering isn't an easy road, and you may not always understand what is happening. That is why it is important to just have faith. After all, Matthew 21:22 tells us, *"And whatever you ask in prayer, you will receive, if you have faith"* (ESV). I also find comfort in Hebrews 11:1, which says, *"Now faith is the assurance of things hoped for, the conviction of things not seen"* (ESV).

AN EXAMPLE OF GOD'S LOVE

Like Tammy, we can all be examples for our child's birth parents. For birth parents and family members, you might be the best example of what a good parent is. Everything you do as a foster parent will send signals to the biological parents on how a parent should act as well as how to treat their own children. Indeed, you are an example of not only how a parent should act, but you are also an example of Christ. As Christians, we are to share our faith with everyone we meet. As foster parents, we can do this sharing in quiet, silent ways, and without breaking any policies about faith that your child welfare system might have in place.

To begin with, we can simply model being a good parent and a

Christian by staying positive and keeping a good attitude, even in the midst of trying times and difficult challenges. I remember a time when a birth parent was cursing at me in front of the caseworker, calling me horrible names and making false accusations against my wife and me about how we were treating her child. The caseworker was relatively new at her job, did nothing to intervene on my behalf, and instead sat there next to me and allowed the birth parent to continue in her attacks. At first, I felt my blood pressure rise, my heart began to race, and I wanted to lash out in defense. Instead, I folded my hands together, and prayed silently to myself, "Love is patient, love is kind," from 1 Corinthians 13:4. When the birth mother rose from the table where we were sitting and spat in my face, I prayed even harder and remained calm. Can I be honest with you? It wasn't very easy for me. Without a doubt, though, it would have only created more problems if I had met her attack with one of my own. I would also not have honored the foster child in my home by treating the child's mother in such a fashion.

Not only can we stay positive and keep a good attitude, but we can also treat our foster child's birth parents with the same dignity, respect, and kindness that Jesus would show. One of the best ways we can show our Christian faith is by treating everyone we meet with these attributes, even if they are not returned. Remember the story of the Good Samaritan that Jesus told when tested by an expert in the law in the tenth chapter of Luke? Let me share it with you.

One afternoon, a young man was traveling from Jerusalem to Jericho. The distance between the two cities is roughly 15 miles and, in the days of Jesus, the roads were very rough and not easy to travel. For this young man, it would have been an all-day trip, taking around eight hours to complete. The road was a popular one for robbers and thieves, as there were many places for them to lie in hiding, waiting to ambush the unsuspecting traveler. Indeed, as our young man was traveling along, he was attacked by a band of robbers, who beat him to within an inch of his life and took all he possessed, including his clothing.

As our young traveler was lying in a ditch, bleeding and broken, a priest happened to pass by him. Looking down upon the wounded traveler, the priest quickly walked to the other side of the road and continued on past him, giving the wounded young man neither love nor compassion, and failed to help him nor involve himself with the traveler. If there was anyone who would have helped the man in the ditch, surely it would have been this man of God, the priest, who would have been well versed in God's law of love. Yet, despite this background, the priest passed by, leaving the beaten man alone.

A little while later, a second man passed by the wounded and bleeding young man who was lying in the ditch waiting for help. This second man was a Levite. Now, all priests were Levites, as priests were selected from the tribe of Levi, but not all Levites were priests. Those Levites that were not priests were assigned duties and responsibilities within the Temple, or place of worship. Along with this responsibility, Levites assisted the priests with various tasks. It is most likely that the Levite passing by the beaten traveler was well aware of his religious call to help others in distress and to bring love and compassion on behalf of someone in need. Yet like the priest, the Levite did the exact same thing. Crossing to the other side of the road, he hurried past the bleeding man, failing to offer any kind of aid whatsoever.

Time passed, and the traveler who was attacked by the gang of robbers continued to suffer, and his condition worsened. The young man was so beaten that he was unable to rise, unable to help himself. As a result, he simply lay in the ditch waiting either for help or for death, whichever might come first. Help did come in the guise of a third traveler, the Good Samaritan. In Jesus's day, Samaritans were despised and hated by the Jewish people for a number of reasons, including the fact that Samarians did not keep all of God's law. In fact, Jews so despised Samaritans that they looked upon the people of Samaria as the worst of the human race and wanted nothing to do with them.

Yet our Samaritan did keep God's law. Looking down upon the beaten traveler, this enemy of the Jewish people did what the priest and the Levite did not do; he looked down, stopped, and helped the man. Seeing a man in desperate need of help, the Samaritan bent down and attended to the traveler's wounds. Using wine to disinfect the wounds and oil to soothe the pain, the Samaritan then dressed the wounds, all in an effort to comfort the beaten traveler. After this care, the Good Samaritan placed the traveler upon his donkey, taking him to the nearest inn. Going beyond what was expected of him, and beyond common decency, the Samaritan paid for a room for the traveler so he could recuperate and find rest and also paid the innkeeper to take care of the wounded traveler. Furthermore, the Samaritan also assured the innkeeper that he would pay any extra expenses when he returned from his trip. Surely, this Good Samaritan saw the wounded and bloody traveler not as someone to ignore but as his neighbor, not as his enemy but as his friend.

As Jesus told this story to those listening, He brought to light a strong contrast between those people who knew the law and those who put it into practice in their life with their actions and with their deeds. Jesus then asked a lawyer, "Which of these three do you think was a neighbor to the man who fell into the hands of robbers?" (Luke 10:36). When the lawyer recognized the truth behind the story, he answered by noting that the third traveler was a neighbor by showing mercy upon the wounded man. When Jesus heard the lawyer's response, He commanded him with this powerful directive: "Go and do likewise" (v. 37).

Go and do likewise. This call is what we are to do with the birth parents of our foster children. This call is what we are to do with those who have abused, abandoned, or neglected the children in our care. Jesus tells us in this parable that we are to follow the Samaritan's example of helping those in need and of showing love and compassion to even those who might consider us their enemies, and vice versa. Like the Good Samaritan showed us in this parable, we are also to love others, regardless of their background.

The Strength of Forgiveness

One evening as we were getting ready to sit down for dinner, my wife and I took a phone call from our child welfare agency. At that time, we had a personal policy of only fostering children who were no older than our oldest child. This situation was the first time we broke that family rule. At that time, our oldest was ten years old, and the child in need was a 13-year-old boy abandoned by his mother. After some time together in prayer listening to God's will for us, I called the case worker back and told her that we would take the child on the condition that he would have to leave our home if he were to cause any problems or be a negative influence upon our own children. Both my wife and I were a little hesitant about taking in a teenaged boy and were concerned that it might not be the best decision for our family.

LOVING YOUR CHILD'S BIRTH PARENTS

When the teenager arrived, I was taken aback at how scared and frightened he was. He looked like a deer in headlights and was obviously terrified about his situation and his surroundings. My wife and I felt so very sad for him and tried to comfort him as best as we could. Perhaps the saddest thing about his situation was how he came into care. His mother had abandoned him under a highway overpass outside of a very busy Atlanta, Georgia. Apparently, his mother had pulled the car over to the side of the road, asked him to get out and get something out of the car's trunk, and then sped off, leaving him alone. When he arrived at our house the next evening, he was nervous, afraid, and anxious. He said very little to us, except to note that his birthday was the next morning. As Kelly and I lay in our bed late that evening, we could hear him crying himself to sleep.

I felt anger toward his mother, outraged that she could abandon her own son on a busy highway, outraged that she did so just before his birthday. My stomach churned with anger, and the emotion clouded my outlook on everything else. It took my wife to remind me that his mother was a child of God herself and needed forgiveness for her actions. After I spent some time in prayer, and with God's grace, I was able to forgive her, which helped me as well.

> Love and forgiveness are intertwined actions that cannot be separated. If we truly love as God asks us to love, then we need to forgive as well. Without forgiveness, there is no love. When I was angry toward our foster teen's mother, I was in no way sharing God's love.

Love and forgiveness are intertwined actions that cannot be separated. If we truly love as God asks us to love, then we need to forgive as well. Without forgiveness, there is no love. When I was angry toward our foster teen's mother, I was in no way sharing God's love. Instead, my stomach was in knots, and I was one tense parent. I was shackled by my own inability to forgive someone, a prisoner to a debilitating emotion. Yet when I did forgive her, it felt like a weight was taken off my own shoulders. One of the amazing things about the act of forgiving others is that it allows us to use our energies toward something that is more constructive, more positive. Forgiveness frees us from the forces of hate and evil and instead allows us to draw closer to God and gives us more strength to do Jesus' work. When we forgive the actions of our foster child's birth parents, we not only show God's love to them and empower ourselves but we also honor our foster children. Remember, these children, despite the many forms of abuse to which they have been subjected, still love their mommies and daddies. Scripture tells us several times that forgiveness is important to our relationship with God.

> FOR IF YOU FORGIVE OTHER PEOPLE WHEN THEY SIN AGAINST YOU, YOUR HEAVENLY FATHER WILL ALSO FORGIVE YOU. BUT IF YOU DO NOT FORGIVE OTHERS THEIR SINS, YOUR FATHER WILL NOT FORGIVE YOUR SINS.
> —MATTHEW 6:14–15

> GET RID OF ALL BITTERNESS, RAGE AND ANGER, BRAWLING AND SLANDER, ALONG WITH EVERY FORM OF MALICE. BE KIND AND COMPASSIONATE TO ONE ANOTHER, FORGIVING EACH OTHER, JUST AS IN CHRIST GOD FORGAVE YOU.
> —EPHESIANS 4:31–32

> THEN PETER CAME TO JESUS AND ASKED, "LORD, HOW MANY TIMES SHALL I FORGIVE MY BROTHER OR SISTER WHO SINS AGAINST ME? UP TO SEVEN TIMES?" JESUS ANSWERED, "I TELL YOU, NOT SEVEN TIMES, BUT SEVENTY-SEVEN TIMES." —MATTHEW 18:21–22

OTHER WAYS TO HELP

As foster parents, we have the opportunity to help not only children in need but their parents as well. As we have seen, we can lift birth parents up in prayer and forgive their actions and crimes against the very children we share in common. There are a number of other ways we can help our foster child's biological family members and act as God's servants.

It may be that your foster child's birth parents are not attending a church. One way you can help them is to invite them to worship with you at your own church. Allow phone calls between your foster child and his birth parents, with you monitoring the calls to ensure that your child remains safe and that neither party says something that is inappropriate. Use video chat to allow your foster child and the birth parents to communicate face to face. Invite the birth parents and biological family members to school events and extracurricular activities. Send school progress reports, report cards, and school projects to the birth parents, allowing them to see the progress their child is making. Ask birth parents to help out with birthday plans for the child.

I discuss some of these best practices in my book *The Foster Parenting Manual*:

> *When your foster child meets with his birth parents for visitations, he should be well dressed, clean, healthy, and looking his best.*

> *Part of your mission [as a foster parent] is to support reunification with the foster child and his biological parents. Do your best to encourage reunification between the child and his parents. Find ways you can help the biological parents with their parenting skills. Discuss ways and ideas on how you can help them work on their case plan, as they attempt to meet the requirements of reunification.*

> *Your foster child's family members will want to know what kind of family their child is living with, what his home life will be like, if he is being taken care of, and many other concerns. After all, their child has been taken away from them against their wishes and placed in a strange home. They will have many concerns and may not be as courteous to you as you might like. Be prepared for them to be hostile, rude, angry, or even distant. Remember, they are hurting and have been through a traumatic experience with the removal of their child. Respectfully encourage them to ask you as many questions as they would like. It is important that you answer their questions as honestly and as openly as possible, treating them with the utmost integrity, kindness, and politeness.*

As a foster parent, it is important to remember that your foster child's biological parents are people in need, and they deserve your kindness and sympathy, not your anger. After all, God calls us to treat others with kindness and compassion rather than with anger, regardless of what we think others might deserve. By working with birth parents and showing them kindness and compassion, you not only help the birth parents but you also teach your foster child an important lesson in love and humanity and what it looks like to walk with Christ.

HEARTBREAK AND LOSS: WHEN YOUR FOSTER CHILD LEAVES

Four-year-old Sally and her six-month-old sister, Jessie, had been with us for four months, our first placement as foster parents. Placed into foster care due to parental drug abuse and neglect, the two children certainly added to our home and our family. Our own three children were roughly the same age as Sally as they ranged between three and six years of age. Sally was rough and often misbehaved, while little Jessie suffered from fetal alcohol syndrome and slept very little at night. We were quickly tired from the two additional children as they brought with them challenges and tests that we had not experienced before. Yet we also quickly grew to love them dearly, and the two girls became part of our own family. Our first placement was on track to becoming permanent placements in our home.

It was a Friday afternoon when my wife got the call. Now, I imagine you are probably familiar with "the call." The call impacts our lives as foster parents in one of two ways. We either receive a call from our child welfare agent asking if we will take into our home a foster child or the caseworker calls to let us know that our foster child will soon be leaving our home. On this particular Friday, it was the latter; Sally and Jessie were leaving our home to move in with their grandparents. It was our first experience with foster children leaving our home, and we soon found that despite our several months of initial foster parent training, we were not prepared for the grief that would soon enter into our home.

"Hi, Mrs. DeGarmo, this is Stephanie," the girls' caseworker said when Kelly answered the phone late that Friday evening. "The girls are going to go and live with their grandparents. We should be there to pick them up Monday after school. Will that be a good time for you?"

My wife hesitated, taking in a deep breath before answering. The call was unexpected, and the news was a bit of a shock. "Yes," she paused, forcing the reply out. Taking another deep breath, my wife went on, "Yes, that will be fine." After getting a few more details and information from the caseworker, Kelly hung up the phone, turning her eyes toward me. I could see the shock and sadness now beginning to settle in. She relayed the conversation to me, and I felt the shock descend upon me as well.

Kelly divided the rest of that weekend between preparing for the girls to leave and trying to hold back the tears that were brought by the grief of losing the two children. We were both so very stunned by the lack of time we were given in advance. As I pointed out to Kelly a number of times that weekend and over the course of the next several months, the girls were going to a good home, to the grandparents—it did little to help. For the next few weeks and months, the pain we felt in our hearts was heavy, it felt as if we were losing our own children.

When a Child Leaves

Perhaps one of the most painful aspects we experience as foster parents is when our foster child leaves our home. Your home becomes a place where your foster children come for a period of time with the goal of being reunited with their family in the near future. After all, we are following God's call to help not just the child but the biological family as well. There are those times, though, when reunification with the birth family is sadly not possible for some foster children, and the birth parents' rights are terminated. Sometimes, these children become available for adoption, and some foster parents do indeed end up making their foster child a permanent addition to their family. We will examine this practice later in chapter 8. My wife and I have adopted three children from foster care during the years and have tried unsuccessfully to adopt others as well. If reunification is not possible with the birth parents, many foster children are instead placed into a birth family member's home. No matter the reason, reunification can be a difficult time for foster parents, leaving us grief stricken, shocked, and even in a state of depression as the child we have come to love as our own leaves our home and our family.

I devote an entire chapter in my book *The Foster Parenting Manual* on the experiences of when a child leaves your care. In it, I state, "Each foster child is different, and each placement into a home creates different sets of emotions. As a foster parent, there may be those children you do not have strong attachments to, due to emotional or behavioral issues, yet an attachment with these children is still made nonetheless." Now, I know that it is not always easy. I have had my fair share of difficult times and challenging children. "Some foster children will be so difficult that you may even ask for them to be removed. Still, other foster children will steal your heart and will become a dear and cherished member of your family, leaving you heartbroken." It will be times like these when it feels like your world is falling apart, your heart is being broken in a thousand pieces, and your life will never be the same. Indeed, as my own experience has shown me over the years, despite the level of attachment, our family, including our departing foster child, has experienced a range of emotion each time it comes time to say good-bye.

I can assure you, my friend, as foster parents we do feel grief during the removal of a foster child from our home as the child has come to be an important and loved member of their family. I meet foster parents all over the nation who tell me their stories of grief when a child in foster care leaves their home for another. Whenever a loved one leaves home, emotions of grief and sadness are normal. There are those other times, though, when you might be angry with the removal. You might believe that the new home where the child is moving is unsafe, unstable, and even unhealthy for him. I have felt this way, and it has left me feeling angry, confused, sad, and concerned. I have to remind myself in situations like these that I am not in charge of the situation, as difficult as it may be. The removal of foster children from a home is often a decision that is made in the court.

I have a bit of bad news for you. It really does not get any easier each time that children move from your home and leave your family. But guess what? It shouldn't get any easier. This emotion is how it really should be. If you experience grief and loss when your foster child leaves, this pain is a reflection of the love that developed between you and your child, a reflection of the love that you gave a child in need. As you know, children in foster care need us to love them; they need us to feel for them. When they leave our homes, we should grieve for them, as it simply means that we have given them what they need the most: our love.

I have watched more than 45 children come to live with me and my family and then move to other homes. Each time, my wife and I have grown to love these children, caring for them as if they were our very own and treating them the same as all the others in our home: biological, adoptive, or foster. Each time a child leaves, my wife and I experience a great sense of loss, even when we can be comforted with the knowledge that the children have gone to a good and safe home. There have been times when my wife has sunk into deep grief, crying for days. We have both spent considerable time on our knees lifting up a former foster child in prayer and asking that God keep a child safe, free from harm, and in a home that loves him. There have also been those times when we felt a small sense of relief when a child left our home. A few years back, we had a sibling group of three children in diapers, all with challenging behaviors and conditions. For those four months, we were run ragged, worn out, and tired. When the children left our home to return to their mother, both my wife and I cried. At the same time, though, we felt that a burden had been lifted off of our shoulders, we could breathe and relax a little, and we could focus on our own children some more.

> " *If you experience grief and loss when your foster child leaves, this pain is a reflection of the love that developed between you and your child, a reflection of the love that you gave a child in need.*

RENEE'S STORY

It was unusually warm for a winter's day. I remember the weather clearly. My husband Scott and I were sitting in a pizza restaurant in our neighborhood with our foster daughter waiting for a call that would either make our dreams come true or break our hearts. We had known for a few weeks that this court date was coming, and we knew that the outcome would likely be another gut wrenching good-bye. But we were foolishly hoping against hope for a last minute reprieve. Our food tasted like cardboard. We looked at each other frequently, trying not to cry, feeling like someone had told us our kid had a terminal illness and had only weeks to live. We were waiting for the awful inevitable end.

Our foster daughter Elizabeth had been with us from birth and was now nearly a year old. In that year, not one person—mother, father, grandparent, or relative—inquired, visited, or made contact. It looked as if she was truly orphaned and would be with us for a very long time. We loved her deeply and could hardly bring ourselves to believe that a few short weeks ago the direction of her case had completely changed and we'd likely be saying good-bye in a few hours. But this is foster care. This was what Christ had called us to. The call came. The news fell hard. The tears fell harder.

In every way, Elizabeth had become part of our family and extended family, of our neighborhood, and of our church. Her loss left many of us grieving. I've often said that losing a foster child is like divorce and death rolled into one. It is like death because the loss and the grief are just as real. It can be like divorce because no one died, but a family has just been torn apart and nothing will ever be the same again. And like divorce, the impact ripples out to everyone. This was certainly true with our ten-year-old nephew Marcus.

He took Elizabeth's leaving particularly hard. He had been part of her daily life. He couldn't completely process the complexities of foster care, and he was hurt and angry. He could hardly look at me, and when we accepted placement of another baby girl a week after Elizabeth left, he refused to look at her, hold her, or even acknowledge her. I understood, but his mom kept apologizing, saying, "Give him time to come around."

About a month after Elizabeth left, I managed to get a little free time. I picked Marcus up from school and took him to his favorite restaurant. We sat down and I said, "Buddy, you know we need to talk."

He took a deep breath and to his credit, he looked me in the eye and said, "OK."

"Marcus, I have a real problem here. The Lord has called Uncle Scott and me to be foster parents. We have to obey. We can't stop, but I almost can't live with knowing that our choice is bringing you so much pain. I don't know what to do."

"But it's too hard for you and for Uncle Scott and for everyone. Elizabeth left and it's not fair!" His voice quivered when he said it, but he managed to stay brave.

"Actually Marcus," I said. "Here's what's not fair. We have everything. We have family. We have the Lord. We have tons of clothes and way too much food. We live in lovely homes in a nice neighborhood surrounded by people who love us, celebrate us, pray for us, and look out for us, while way too many children have none of these things. How can we not take what God has blessed us with and give to kids who need us? We're Christians, Marcus, and this is what Christ calls us to do even if it hurts. It's not about our pain. It's about taking the pain of the foster kids."

He was silent for a full minute or two, and I could tell he was letting this sink in. Then, with tears rolling down his face he said, "It's what Christ did for us on the Cross. It's what we have to do. I can do it, too."

"Marcus, are you sure?" I asked.

"Yes, I can do it," he answered.

And he did! I can still see it clear as day in my mind's eye. Marcus and I were in the car with one of our many foster babies. We were taking this precious boy to meet his aunt who had been approved to be his kinship caregiver, and we were facing another hard good-bye. Marcus had insisted on coming with me and riding in the backseat with Ritchie. Ritchie had been shaken at three months and suffered a broken arm, bleeding brain, and cracked ribs. Many prayers had gone up for this sweet boy, and miraculously he was on the mend. As we neared our destination, Marcus asked me if we had time to stop for a minute. Thinking he wanted to say good-bye, I pulled over. But to my surprise, he said he wanted to pray for Ritchie. I cried as I listened from the front seat to this beautiful prayer: "God thank You so much for giving us Ritchie for a short time. Thank You for letting us love him. Thank You for healing him. Walk with him all of his life and let him know he's loved. Thank You for giving us the strength to say good-bye. Help us love our next foster baby just as much. Amen."

Thank you, Marcus. I couldn't have prayed it better myself.

RELYING ON GOD IN TIMES OF GRIEF

Grief is a natural part of life and is common to all who love and experience loss. Indeed, God provides us with many examples in His Word of people who have experienced grief and loss. People such as Job, Naomi, Hannah, and David all suffered deep sadness from the trials that these Old Testament characters experienced. Along with them, the Son of God, Jesus Christ, also experienced grief when Lazarus, the brother of Martha and Mary, died. When Jesus heard the news and watched those who knew and loved Lazarus mourn, Jesus also grieved. One of my friend's favorite verses in the Bible is John 11:35. The verse is a short one, only two words long, yet it gives us all great insight into our Lord. The verse simply says, "Jesus wept." This verse, these two words, should comfort us, as He sympathizes with our own pain.

There is nothing wrong with grieving; it is a natural part of the human condition. At some point in our lives, we will all grieve. Even more likely is that we will all experience grief multiple times in our lives. As foster parents, you may experience feelings of grief and loss each time a foster child leaves your home, though the degree of this grief may likely vary with each child. Truly, God expects us to grieve and encourages us to do so. Grief can allow us to pause and reflect upon a loved one and on our perspective on life. God reminds us throughout Scripture that time helps the hurt of grief to subside.

WEEPING MAY STAY FOR THE NIGHT, BUT
REJOICING COMES IN THE MORNING. —PSALM 30:5

A TIME TO WEEP AND A TIME TO LAUGH, A TIME
TO MOURN AND A TIME TO DANCE. —ECCLESIASTES 3:4

When our first child died from a disease known as anencephaly, a condition where the brain fails to develop, both my wife and I were devastated. We both reacted differently to the loss of our first child. Kelly grieved in a healthy fashion, while I did not. I remained in denial for quite some time, in fact, for the next two years. I buried myself in my work, refusing to grieve or feel sadness. It was not healthy for either me or for our marriage. Looking back at this time in my life years later, I have come to realize that people experience grief in different ways. As Christians, we can all find strength and comfort in God's word while we experience grief. Certainly, there are many Scripture verses that remind us that we can turn to God during these times of deep sadness. As foster parents, these are verses we can turn to time and time again when a child leaves our home and when we grieve this time of loss.

The LORD is close to the brokenhearted and saves those who are crushed in spirit. —Psalm 34:18

Blessed are those who mourn, for they will be comforted. —Matthew 5:4

Come to me, all you who are weary and burdened, and I will give you rest. —Matthew 11:28

Humble yourselves, therefore, under God's mighty hand, that he may lift you up in due time. Cast all your anxiety on him because he cares for you. —1 Peter 5:6–7

So do not fear, for I am with you; do not be dismayed, for I am your God. I will strengthen you and help you; I will uphold you with my righteous right hand. —Isaiah 41:10

For no one is cast off by the LORD forever. Though he brings grief, he will show compassion, so great is his unfailing love. For he does not willingly bring affliction or grief to anyone. —Lamentations 3:31–33

Praise be to the God and Father of our Lord Jesus Christ, the Father of compassion and the God of all comfort, who comforts us in all our troubles, so that we can comfort those in any trouble with the comfort we ourselves receive from God. —2 Corinthians 1:3–4

"He will wipe every tear from their eyes. There will be no more death" or mourning or crying or pain, for the old order of things has passed away. —Revelation 21:4

Stages of Grief

In my book *The Foster Parenting Manual,* I discuss how saying good-bye to a child in your care creates its own kind of grief.

Grief can be expressed in a variety of ways, depending upon the individual, as it is a personal experience. Some will shed tears and cry, while others will hold their pain inside. Some will busy themselves in a task, while others will seem detached and far away. The departure of your foster child from your home can be one that is devastating to you and your family. A brief look at the stages of grief, based upon [Dr. Elisabeth] Kübler-Ross's work of 1969, is important in order to understand fully the feelings that may come along with the removal of your foster child from your family. These same feelings may have been felt by your foster child when he was removed from his own home and first placed in yours.

SHOCK: The removal of the foster child may bring feelings of shock to the foster family. After a family member has formed an emotional attachment to the child, the sudden removal may cause deep shock and uncertainty, leaving the foster family confused.

DENIAL: With a sudden departure, some foster parents may deny that they ever formed a relationship with their foster child or feel any sadness toward the removal. Even though they deny these feelings, they grieve, believing that they were unable to provide the help the child needed.

ANGER: A foster child's removal from a foster parent home may bring feelings of anger and severe disappointment with the caseworker as well as with the child welfare agency system. Foster parents may blame the system or caseworker for the placement of their foster child into an environment they feel is not productive or is even harmful to the child.

GUILT: During this stage, foster parents may experience feelings of guilt, blaming themselves with the belief that they are at fault, and try to comprehend what they did "wrong" in the removal of the foster child. Still other foster parents may experience guilt if they were the ones asking for the removal, as they were unable to continue caring for the child.

BARGAINING: Some foster parents will try to substitute the grief they have with helping others in need in an attempt to justify the loss of their foster child. Others will try to substitute the loss with the placement of another foster child in their home, hoping that this new placement will help them forget about the child that just left.

DEPRESSION: There are different components to depression brought on by grief. Some foster parents will become easily irritated; others will experience a constant state of feeling tired. Others will feel as if they can no longer continue with their day-to-day lives and have a difficult time with the tasks associated with family, friends, work, and marriage.

ACCEPTANCE: After the passage of time, the grief from the loss of the foster child decreases, allowing the foster parent to accept the removal of the child and move on. The emotional well-being of the foster parent improves, and a sense of understanding of the child's removal becomes clearer.

SELF HELP DURING TIMES OF GRIEF

As you know, the power of prayer is a mighty one. It is also a gift from God that allows us to commune with Him, to spend time with Him, and to be a part of His will. When you experience feelings of grief and loss after a child leaves your home, you can find comfort in the presence of God through the act of prayer.

There are other ways that you can also find relief from the pain you are feeling after a child moves from your home. One of the most important steps you can take to aid in this time of loss is to surround yourself with a support group. As we have seen, many times foster parent associations fill this role, as they provide fellow foster parents who have undergone the same displacement, or removal of a child, within their own homes. Churches and loved ones may also provide this type of support. Within these groups, foster parents will have the opportunity to express their grief without feelings of embarrassment or judgment. Indeed, as one of the stages of grief is that of anger, grieving foster parents can release their anger to members of these support groups.

Many foster parents choose to put their feelings of loss and grief to paper and pen, writing down their emotions in a journal or diary. This journaling allows the grieving foster parent the opportunity to release their feelings in a more private manner, yet release them nevertheless. To be sure, if feelings of loss and grief are not given the opportunity to be released, they will become suppressed, which may later lead to further complications such as depression, anxiety, and other health-related problems. With this risk in mind, it is most important for foster parents to recognize that they may be experiencing loss and to face these feelings in some fashion.

For some, grief and loss may lead to physical health issues such as stress, fatigue, and tension. Regular exercise and healthy eating habits are essential in combating these issues. During this time of loss, it is also important that foster parents ensure that they are getting enough sleep, as lack of proper rest will also result in stress and fatigue. Specific calendar dates may also trigger overwhelming feelings of grief and loss. Birthdays, holidays, and certain milestones for the foster child and family may revive memories and feelings. Foster parents suffering from loss need to be aware of this potential beforehand and prepare themselves for these feelings.

If you do have contact with your former foster child, consider reaching out to the child. After all, it is likely that the child will be missing his former foster family as well. Again, I state in *The Foster Parenting Manual*:

> *To help him [as well as yourself] in this time of transition, it is important to reach out and contact him. Call him on the phone and allow him to tell you all about his new home and new family. Encourage your own children to speak with him as well. Write letters to him and send him pictures of your family and family events from time to time. Remember birthdays and other important events in his life, including holidays and school events, and send cards. If you live nearby, let him know when you can attend school functions and extra-curricular activities or programs of his. If possible, arrange visits for him to come to your house. Not only will he enjoy it, but his new [or biological] family may certainly appreciate the break as well.*

Saying good-bye is never easy for anyone and may be especially diffi-cult for you and your foster child. After your foster child leaves your home, you may feel like you never wish to foster again, as the pain is too great. The grief you feel may be overwhelming.

Please remember this reassurance though, my friend: you are not alone. There is a God above who is delighted that you are taking care of children in need, His children. So lift up your foster children in prayer to Him when they leave your home. Take time to grieve, and remind yourself that you are not in control of the situation. God is in control always, and He is good!

A FOREVER FAMILY

The goal of foster care is a forever family, by way of reunification with the birth parents, adoption into the family that has been fostering the child, or adoption into another home. John shared his family's journey in foster care and adoption with me.

JOHN'S STORY

About seven years ago, my wife and I decided to embark on the foster-to-adopt journey. My wife knew nothing about fostering, but I, as a second-generation foster parent, understood some of what to expect. We decided to go into fostering in the hopes of adopting a school-aged boy. We had two older children ready to graduate from school and so much more love to give that it just seemed like the right thing to do.

Our first placement was a sibling group of three, the oldest of whom my wife knew from her school. The children ranged from the ages of seven years to 18 months, two girls and a boy. We thought this was a perfect fit, and after two months of taking care of them, we thought we would be able to adopt the children. We went to court and found out that the mother was being deported, the father was not on the birth certificate, and the boyfriend of the mother was going to jail for molestation of the oldest daughter. The last time we went to court for the children, we were asked to bring them with us because an aunt in Texas said that she would take them. We spoke with the CASA worker, and he said that it wasn't the ideal place but that they would be with family. This was certainly not what we wanted to hear, but we took them to court. It seemed like everything was moving way too fast. The judge ordered the children to go with the aunt, who the child welfare agency had paid to come from Texas to Georgia for the court hearing. After the court session was over, the children's caseworker got on the phone and purchased the children and aunt's tickets to Texas. They were going to Texas immediately. We drove the children to the bus station and stayed with them until they got on the bus. Watching them go with a stranger they did not know was the most heart-wrenching thing we have ever done. I can still hear the 18-month girl screaming "Mommy" to my wife with her arms stretched out and tears streaming down her face. My wife turned to me crying and said, "I can't do this again."

After a few weeks and a lot of prayer on my part, my wife began to answer the calls for placements again. After a few placements, we were asked if we would take twin premature girls. This was not what we signed up for at all. We wanted a school-aged boy, but my wife called me up and told me to meet her at a nearby store because we had twin newborn girls. The girls were actually 16 days old and two weeks premature. We found out their names, and that was about it. The caseworker that was in charge of them had resigned, and they were placed with us during the holiday season. It was very hard finding out any information about the children until after the holidays were over. We were blessed by God all the way around in this situation.

The girls' biological parents were meth addicts. The father was in jail the first six months of their placement with us. The mother seemed to be making some progress, which worried us, because we fell in love with these girls. Once the father was released from jail, everything changed. The child welfare agency was doing everything in their power it seemed to make things work for the biological parents and not caring what was best for the children. I asked the caseworker why that was, and she told me something that changed my whole outlook on the situation. She told me that the child welfare agency had to do everything in their power to ensure that they were able to stand up in court and tell the judge that there was nothing else they could do, that the parents simply were not willing to work their case plan. I went home and prayed a lot after that for the next six months. In October, the parents had enough and decided to terminate their parental rights. We were very happy to hear this, and I had to thank God. He was looking out for our girls. A few months after the biological parents terminated their rights, we adopted the girls, and they are four and a half today. They are the blessing that God gave us, and we will never forget it.

We closed our home after we adopted the girls, but the passion for helping foster children never left me. I was elected president of the Cobb County Foster Adoptive Parents Association. Our association holds monthly meetings where our foster parents receive a community-donated meal, free child care, and training for the mandated hours the state gives for continuing education. Before my first term, a Baptist church hosted us, but we began to outgrow it. We moved our meetings to our local Presbyterian church where we have been for three years now. The Presbyterian church helped us become more organized and continue to grow. It is a blessing that we are able to depend on a church with such a large heart to help care for our children and foster families on a monthly basis.

ADOPTION THROUGH FOSTER CARE

Over the years, my own family has been blessed with the gift of adopting three children from foster care. These have been joyous events for my family, but there were also times of great anxiety, too, when it appeared that the adoptions might not go through as first planned. Fortunately, all three adoptions did take place, and my wife and I are now the loving parents of six children. Three of these are biological; three are adopted.

I discuss in my book *The Foster Parenting Manual* some of what to expect when adopting through foster care.

When a child is . . . placed into a foster care home, the intent is that the placement is temporary, with reunification the main objective. Yet, there are those instances when reunification is not possible, and the child is placed through the court system for adoption.

Of the over 560,000 children placed in foster care in the United States in 2010, it is estimated that 107,000 become eligible for adoption. Sadly, only around 53,000 of these children were adopted during that year, with over half of these children being adopted by foster parents, with the rest being adopted by family members, and a small percentage being adopted by non-relatives (AFCARS 2012). Nearly 60 percent of children in foster care in America wait two or more years before being adopted.

For those children who are not adopted, many remain in the foster care system for extended periods of time. Some of these children are moved to group homes, while others simply age out of the foster care system, never truly finding a family of their own and a place to call home.

There are several reasons why a foster child might be placed up for adoption. First, custody rights of the birth parents are voluntarily terminated; second, the custody rights of the birth parents are terminated by a court order; and third, the child is up for adoption due to the death of birth parents.

Recently, child welfare agencies have found that foster parents are the ideal people to adopt a foster child. After all, the foster family has been raising the child for an extended amount of time, meeting his needs and nurturing him since he was removed from his birth parents' home. If he has special needs, the foster parents are familiar with these and have gained valuable insight and resources on how best to meet these needs.

Adoption by foster parents will also allow him to remain in the same school system, benefiting from having the same teachers who are already familiar with him and his needs. The child is familiar with his foster parents and has formed a strong and meaningful attachment to them during the course of his placement within their home.

If you are like me, our foster children often become members of our families, and when they are able legally to stay with us, there is a time of rejoicing.

GOD'S CALL TO ADOPT

My favorite character in the Bible is Paul, from the New Testament. I am in awe of how God used such a fallen person as Paul, or Saul as he was known before changing his name. Saul was an enemy to God before his life changing experiences led him to become one of the greatest witnesses for Christ that ever lived. Despite the many attacks Saul led against Christians, a loving God adopted him into His family. Paul writes about this adoption in the Book of Ephesians:

> GOD DECIDED IN ADVANCE TO ADOPT US INTO HIS OWN FAMILY
> BY BRINGING US TO HIMSELF THROUGH JESUS CHRIST. THIS IS WHAT HE
> WANTED TO DO, AND IT GAVE HIM GREAT PLEASURE.
> —EPHESIANS 1:5 NLT

When we adopt a child, we are following God's example; as He has adopted us into His family, so should we do the same with others. The act of adopting a child allows us to be God's hands and feet for those children who have no family to call their own. We also allow God to work through us to use our story of adoption to affect and touch the lives of others. After all, when we adopt a child from foster care, our friends, our family members, our church, and others are watching what we do. This act of changing our family forever may inspire others to do the same. Indeed, I pray that my own children, both biological and adopted, are inspired and called to help others in need when they grow older. Surely God sheds a tear every time a child is harmed, every time a child is abandoned, and every time a child is orphaned. When we adopt a child that has been abused, that has been abandoned, and that needs a family, we are adopting not only for ourselves and for the child, but we are also adopting for Him. After all, God equips us

> *Surely God sheds a tear every time a child is harmed, every time a child is abandoned, and every time a child is orphaned. When we adopt a child that has been abused, that has been abandoned, and that needs a family, we are adopting not only for ourselves and for the child, but we are also adopting for Him.*

with the wisdom, compassion, love, and strength to allow us to bring His children into our own family.

WHEN ADOPTIONS ARE DISRUPTED

Yet, there are those times when adoption through the foster care system does not go as planned. Sadly, sometimes an adoption from foster care is disrupted, hurting all involved. Perhaps your heart was broken when you tried to adopt your foster child. Perhaps you are still grieving this loss. Perhaps you are still trying to comprehend what went wrong. Perhaps you have a story like Lisa and Tony.

Lisa and her husband, Tony, had plans to adopt their foster child, Cooper. Cooper had come to live with the married couple when he was just three months old. The tiny baby had been placed into care for reasons of neglect by his mother, and his father was nowhere to be found at the time. Lisa and Tony grew to love little Cooper and raised him as their own. The couple had decided to become foster parents when they found that they were unable to have children themselves. A year and a half passed, and Cooper's mother lost her rights to her son, leaving the child open for adoption. Lisa and her husband were thrilled, as they had been praying for the opportunity to adopt a child. After meeting with the caseworker, they hired an attorney and began preparing for little Cooper to become part of their family permanently. It seemed as if God had answered their prayers for a child to call their own.

Twenty-one months after Cooper had been placed with his foster parents, Lisa received a call at home from the caseworker one morning. The foster mother and soon-to-be forever mother of little Cooper was stunned to hear that her foster son's birth father had come back into the picture seeking custody of his child. Trying to choke back the tears that threatened to overwhelm her, Lisa listened as the caseworker explained that the child welfare agency would examine the birth father to determine if he could be reunified with his son. Hanging up the phone, Lisa was full of questions and called Tony to share the disturbing news with him. Angry and confused, Tony argued that the birth father had never seen Cooper, let alone formed any kind of relationship with him. After three more months passed, Cooper left Lisa and Tony's home to live with his birth father. Despite the fact that the little foster child had only known Tony and

Lisa as his mother and father, despite the fact that the child, now two years old, had never met his birth father, he was removed from those who knew him and loved him best. The disrupted adoption left Lisa and Tony reeling in confusion. Lisa sank into depression, and Tony grew bitter and angry. The failed adoption created a division in their marriage as they tried to grapple with their own grief.

Perhaps you have a story similar to Robyn and Joe. This foster couple entered into foster care for the sole reason of adopting a child. Like Lisa and Tony, the older couple was unable to have children. After much discussion and prayer together, the two took foster parenting classes to begin their journey as hopeful parents. Shortly after their training ended, Robyn and Joe had a 16-year-old girl by the name of Laura placed in their home. Laura suffered from reactive attachment disorder, a condition that prohibited her from forming healthy relationships with others. The emotionally troubled teen initially came into care after her birth mother and father had both physically and sexually abused her over the course of several years. Along with this abuse, both parents were alcoholics and had a long history of drug abuse.

The first few months of Laura's placement went very well, and Robyn and Joe were quite happy with how their foster teen was fitting into their family. The times where Laura was argumentative and defiant were simply chalked up to normal teenage behavior, so the foster couple thought. Her emotional immaturity was also thought to be a phase out of which she would grow. When the rights of Laura's birth parents were terminated, the couple excitedly rushed into the adoption process, slowing down only to ask Laura if she would like to become part of Robyn and Joe's family forever. Now 17 years old, Laura agreed and soon became part of Robyn and Joe's family.

The honeymoon did not last very long for the family, though. Laura's emotional immaturity only seemed to increase, as did her arguments with Joe. When disciplined, the teen would yell that she wanted to go back home to her birth family, leaving Robyn in tears. Laura continued to misbehave, and upon her eighteenth birthday, the former foster child and adopted daughter of Robyn and Joe quit school, moved out of her new home, and returned back to live with her birth parents. The adoptive parents were devastated emotionally and were only disappointed further when they found out that Laura had become pregnant just four months after she had turned her back on her adoptive parents.

To be sure, there are times in all of our lives when it seems that heartbreak is all around and that our faith might be tested by the very despair we are facing. These times are when we need to rely on our faith more than ever. Choosing to trust in God rather than our feelings may take a great deal of faith. Yet, God reassures us over and over in Scripture that He wants us to come to Him during difficult times, during times of depression, during times of grief and great sadness. God takes our pain and places it upon His own shoulders. Even when we feel as if no one understands us, God is there. Even when we feel that there is no one we can turn to for help, God is there. But when we share our burdens and sadness with Christ, we will find rest. Please allow me to share some of His words with you.

> COME TO ME, ALL YOU WHO LABOR AND ARE HEAVY LADEN, AND I WILL GIVE YOU REST. TAKE MY YOKE UPON YOU AND LEARN FROM ME, FOR I AM GENTLE AND LOWLY IN HEART, AND YOU WILL FIND REST FOR YOUR SOULS. FOR MY YOKE IS EASY AND MY BURDEN IS LIGHT. —MATTHEW 11:28–30 NKJV

CINDY'S STORY

We never wanted to adopt when we became foster parents but quickly understood the devastation that happens in our family when a child that we have been caring for leaves. I didn't think it would be as hard as it proved to be. I learned to compartmentalize in my head to help me cope, but it is still so very hard on the whole family. I would pray hard for God's will to be done in the lives of the children we were caring for. If that meant they left us, then I knew that God had a greater plan, and we were only a small part. I believe that God placed every child that has been in our home. They could have called any other home in our county (and there used to be way more homes than there are now), but for some reason, the child welfare agency called us. People often say, "Those children are so lucky to have you." If they only knew that those children are teaching us, too. I think sometimes God places them in our home not only for us to care for them but for them to help teach us as well. I have to remind myself often that if children stay in my home and don't go home, then there is a birth family that will be devastated. How is my loss any more important than theirs? So when they leave me, as sad as it is, it is a joyful occasion for another family. Maybe the parents didn't get them back, but there may be grandparents who are good people wanting them back desperately. They should have their children just like I would want mine. So again, remembering that God's plan is sovereign, not just for me but also for the birth family, helps me to cope with my loss. To sum it all up, Jesus loves these children and their birth families as much as He loves me and mine.

AFTER ADOPTION

Just because a foster child finds a forever family when he is adopted does not mean that it will be smooth sailing afterwards or that there will not be difficulties or challenges ahead. As a Christian, you can help prevent some of these challenges that your child and your family might face by praying for God to clear anything that might harm your child and your family and that He lead you through this time of growth and change.

Help your former foster child and now permanent member of your family by working with them to understand why the adoption took place and why he has a new family. The internal process for all involved can be a challenging one, especially for your child. He may have a difficult time accepting the fact that he will never return to live with his biological parents or birth family members again. It is necessary for you as an adoptive parent to allow your child time to grieve the loss of connection with his birth family. He may very well need time to experience the stages of grief before he fully transfers attachment from his birth family to yours. Even though he may have lived in your home for some time as a foster child, he will likely re-experience feelings of loss during the adoption process. Allow him to discuss his feelings of grief and loss with you as you listen attentively to him, validating his feelings and emotions. If he should ask any questions about his biological parents or birth family, it is important that you answer them as honestly as you can. At the same time, help him to transfer attachment from his birth family to yours by ensuring that he is included in all aspects of your family, and when possible, incorporate parts of his previous family's traditions into your own, as it helps him to feel more comfortable.

ANDREA'S STORY

God has His will written all over our family's story. At the start of our journey, all we knew was that God wanted us to adopt a sibling group from foster care, but we kept hearing *wait, not at this time, love these children but only until they go home, wait, trust Me, wait.* It wasn't until we finally surrendered to God that we realized that God's plan for us was much bigger than we had ever expected. After several foster placements, God finally said *these are your children.* These children were a sibling group of five. My husband and I fostered them for two years, but shortly after they moved in we realized we were in for the long haul. Life was crazy with four in diapers!

I don't know how we knew it, but God made it very clear we weren't done. We had six years between two of our children, and we knew God had a child that belonged in this space. We inquired about a child about eight months after the adoption was finalized, but the doors shut when we found out we were pregnant with our third biological child. Then after our daughter was born, the unimaginable happened; my health started to fail, and I began to question God. Why, God, would you give me eight children and make me incapable of caring for them? I begged God for answers and eventually found faith to trust God's plan. Two years later we found an answer to my health problems, and everything started to turn around. Shortly after this, God pricked our heart again. Our oldest daughter and I were browsing the pictures of adoptable children from our state's foster care system, and we came to one group of children. The two of us looked at the picture and each other in amazement and called dad over to the computer because we both knew these children belonged in our family. They were another group of five children with striking similarities to our first sibling group.

We inquired about this beautiful group of children but were turned down as they would soon be placed with their new adoptive family. I was heartbroken but had faith that somehow these children would eventually be part of our lives. As time went on, God began to pull my husband and me out of our introverted shells by asking us to speak publicly about the joys of adoption, specifically from foster care. One particular morning we were speaking at a church for their Orphan Sunday and God ripped the floor out from under us. I was seven weeks pregnant at the time with number nine, and as the sermon was given, the same picture that had caught our attention six months earlier popped up on the screen and I heard, "These children have just gone through a terrible disruption and need a loving and understanding family to adopt them." To say the rest was history was an understatement because God used the next nine months of our lives to build our faith in Him.

We were honest and up front that we were expecting but that we felt these children belonged in our home. It would take a whole book of its own to share the wonders that God worked through the process. We fought hard to have our children placed in our home, and we watched God move mountain after mountain to the point that we were able to finalize the adoption exactly five years after our first adoption was finalized! Through the process, in the eyes of many, we became certified members of the loony farm with 14 children living in our home at once.

My husband and I talked, and we were pretty certain we were done for at least a while, but God laughed at these plans. Less than four months after the adoption was finalized, God said *I need you to trust Me and show Me that you believe your children that I brought home to you are indeed My promise that I will set the lonely in families.* Our precious children we had just adopted had a new baby sister, and understanding what we know about sibling connections, we knew it would be in the best interest of all six of them to grow up together. We are up against a foster family who wants to adopt her who will do anything to make it happen.

We have taken action and are trusting that God will bring her home. It hasn't been easy, but we have full faith that God's will can happen, even if we are only along for the ride to bring glory to Him and to be the vessel He uses to accomplish it. Our life isn't easy, and it is even a little bit crazy but through our mustard seed sized faith God has given us a testimony that is hard to ignore.

THE CHURCH AND FOSTER CARE

Recently, I have had the blessing and wonderful opportunity to speak to churches about how God can use them to help children in care. During these occasions, I have witnessed lives changed as God spoke through me and entered into the hearts of those listening. I have seen people moved to tears from the stories I have shared with them about foster children. I have listened as others have told me of their inability to have children of their own and who felt the call to help other children. I have even sat by those who told me through tears about their own experiences when they were abused and abandoned as a child and wanted to help those children today who are experiencing a similar fate. In all these occasions, I have seen others looking for ways to reach out to foster children, seeking ways to protect them.

You see, not everyone is called to be a foster parent. As you know, not everyone has the skills to bring children into their home and care for those in need. To be sure, God gives us all different skills and talents. For some, these talents might be to care for children in their own homes on a day-to-day basis. For others, it might be to support those who care for them, while others might be given the resources from God to share. The Bible is quite specific on the gifts of talents and abilities.

WE HAVE DIFFERENT GIFTS, ACCORDING TO THE GRACE GIVEN TO EACH OF US. IF YOUR GIFT IS PROPHESYING, THEN PROPHESY IN ACCORDANCE WITH YOUR FAITH; IF IT IS SERVING, THEN SERVE; IF IT IS TEACHING, THEN TEACH; IF IT IS TO ENCOURAGE, THEN GIVE ENCOURAGEMENT; IF IT IS GIVING, THEN GIVE GENEROUSLY; IF IT IS TO LEAD, DO IT DILIGENTLY; IF IT IS TO SHOW MERCY, DO IT CHEERFULLY. —ROMANS 12:6–8

As we know, God does call all of His children to care for those in need and gives us all individual talents and abilities to do so. There are amazing ways that God uses the church to help both foster children and foster parents. The first should be obvious: prayer. Children in foster care face danger, darkness, tragedy, and trauma on a daily basis. These children are caught up in what I believe to be a spiritual war as they come under attack from so many different angles. They need people on their side lifting them up in prayer each day from the time the sun comes up to the time they go to bed. Prayer ministries or prayer teams can be instrumental in helping members of a church become more involved not only in helping foster children but in changing the course of their lives. Without a doubt, God hears our prayers and answers them in His way.

There are a number of ways a church can pray for a foster child and his foster family, as we noted in chapter 4. A prayer team can also begin praying for the child even before he is placed into his foster home, praying that the transition is as smooth and as comfortable as possible. Prayer teams can pray for the specific needs of the child and for any obstacles or hurdles that he might have in front of him. Along with these requests, church members can also keep the foster family lifted up in prayer as well, at all times asking that God grant them the strength, wisdom, and compassion they need as they minister to their foster child.

SUPPORT GROUPS
AND VISITATIONS

A few years back, my foster parent association support group felt that we needed to move our monthly meetings to another location. We were meeting each month at our local child welfare agency. Although we appreciated the opportunity to meet there and the willingness of the agency to open their doors to us one evening each month for our training sessions and support group, it was decided that we needed to find another location, one that was more warm and inviting to the foster children in our care. After all, the local child welfare agency was a symbol to them that they were in care, and a reminder that they were not with their own families. Following some prayer about it and discussion with my fellow members of our support group and association, I placed a request to my church and board of elders that our local association use the church's fellowship hall and kitchen facilities for our monthly meetings. The answer the church provided was one that I did not anticipate.

It seemed that my wife and I, along with the other foster parents in our small town, had touched the hearts of many in our congregation with our act of helping our community's children. After discussion in one of the church's committees, the church granted our request to have our monthly meetings within the walls of the church my wife and I had come to love. What is even more helpful, though, is the additional help with which we have been blessed each month at the meetings. Several members of our church volunteer each month to provide our meetings with a cooked meal and child care. For my wife and me, and the other foster parents in our community, it is almost like going out on a date. Our meal is already cooked and prepared, and we have a reprieve from being foster parents, if only for a short time! For an hour or so, several adults in the church scurry the children into play time, arts and crafts, and various other enjoyable activities, leaving us uninterrupted while we attend a foster parenting training session, share resources and information, or just sit around a table laughing and crying together as we share stories. These meetings are ones that both my wife and I look forward to each month, and the members of the support group to which we belong are very grateful for this simple yet tremendous ministry of our church.

> *Churches can provide a safe, consistent, warm, and inviting atmosphere for children and birth family members to meet during visitation sessions.*

Perhaps there is a church in your area that is looking for a way to minister to others. Maybe your own church is seeking ways to reach out to those in need. Hosting a local foster parent association and support group is one such way a church can serve foster parents. Another way is serving as a location for family visitations. Churches can provide a safe, consistent, warm, and inviting atmosphere for children and birth family members to meet during visitation sessions. Not only can this hospitality be a form of outreach for a church, but the message of Christ's love and forgiveness is also being practiced as well. Let's examine what Joanne and her church are doing in Georgia:

> *I am privileged to help coordinate family visitations at our church for children who are in foster care. Every other Saturday our church has volunteers in place, and we set up rooms for children to visit with their birth parents and other family members from 11:00 a.m. to 1:00 p.m. We have space both outside and inside for children and a nursery for little ones. We work with the state's child welfare system to set up the visits but also have a close relationship with foster parents so that we can make sure the children can spend time with their birth parents and other relatives. Children get to play, draw, eat, celebrate birthdays and other holidays, and just talk and be with their parents for two hours. I have noticed that many foster parents have very strong relationships with the birth parents, and it is in these situations that trust is built and children can grow and develop well.*

> *We have seen many families come and go over the years. Some of the families have reunited, but others have not been able to resolve the conflicts in their families. I do believe though that God is working in all these families and that in some small way we are able to provide a safe place for children to be with their families. I recall a case in which a sister and brother would come regularly on Saturdays to be with their grandparents. Every Saturday, their grandmother would have some kind of board game such as chess for the children to play, and their grandfather would talk with them about what they had been doing during the week. The children were always excited to see them and really did not notice that there was even anyone else in the room because they had so many things to share and talk about. On one Saturday, their mother and an aunt also attended the visit and spent time with the children. Eventually, the grandparents were given custody of the children, and the family was reunited.*

> *We thank God for these joys. We do see some sadness where parents just cannot overcome the obstacles in their lives to take care of the children they love on a daily basis, but I do think it helps the children*

*to know on certain Saturdays they can come to our church and be
with their families.*

A Generous Heart and Generous Gifts

There are those times when foster parents require a short-term break
from their foster child. This break may be the result of foster
parents traveling on vacation, a temporary move into a new home, or
the birth children in the foster home requiring some much needed
time with their own parents. This break is often known as respite
care. Respite care may also be used simply because some foster
parents are trying to prevent burn out and need a break from their
foster child. Other foster parents are often used for respite as they
are officially licensed to look after foster children.

In some parts of the nation, there are those foster care and child
welfare agencies that allow others besides foster parents to care for
foster children during times of respite. This respite provision is a
wonderful way for members in a church to reach out and offer
a helping and loving hand, just as Christ would have us do. Volunteers
would be required to receive training from their local child welfare
agency before being able to provide respite care, and a quick phone
call to the agency in your area should allow you to find out all the
information your volunteers and church members would need in
this regard. By providing respite care, your church is not only
helping the children in care but also the foster parents who have
custody of them. This type of involvement by your church could be
a tremendous beacon of God's love. As a foster parent myself, I can
assure you that respite care is often invaluable for both the child and
family in times of need.

There is a lovely couple at my church that has a heart for children
in foster care yet are unable to be foster parents themselves. For
years now they have watched my wife and I take care of dozens of
children, some staying for a few days while others stay for several
months and even years. This couple has been a blessing to my wife
and me each Christmas as they have taken the mantle upon themselves of being our "foster grandparents." Each Christmas season,
they purchase presents for every foster child that is in our house.
This generosity has helped Kelly and me ensure that our children in
foster care have an extra special Christmas Day as we share both the

message and joy of Jesus' birth and the joy of receiving gifts under the tree, gifts with a child's name on them. Sadly, far too many children in foster care have never had gifts to open on December 25. My wife and I try to make it a day that the children never forget and one when they are able to escape their pain and suffering and simply revel in being a child. Our "foster grandparents" help us accomplish this goal. Like our dear friends have done, churches can reach out to the foster parents in their community and "adopt" a child during the holiday season or other times of the year. This provision might also include helping out with school supplies at the beginning of the school year, birthdays, paying for school field trips and summer camps, and other activities that are special to the child. Many foster parents simply cannot afford to provide all of these opportunities to their foster child, opportunities that help their child escape from trauma and heal from their suffering. When church members come together to help the child in such fashion, they are also giving a blessing to the foster parents.

I recently heard from one foster parent who told me that her church was collecting new and gently used suitcases for the foster children in their area. When a child came into care in their community, the church would work alongside the town's foster parent association and make sure that each child received a suitcase. In fact, there are many such organizations across the United States that provide similar services. When a child comes into care, all too often he comes with a black plastic bag containing the few items in his possession, gathered together quickly by social workers and even law enforcement officers in a hurry to collect both the child and his possessions. For older children in care, this black plastic bag can be an embarrassing symbol of all that is wrong in their lives. Later, when a child in foster care moves, whether it is to a new foster home, an adoptive family, or reunited with his birth family, the gift of a new suitcase can be a sign of pride, respect, and love.

A few years ago, I had the privilege of interviewing Leigh Esau for a magazine article. Leigh has created an amazing program for the foster children in her area and is a great model for others who are looking for ways to help share God's love with children in care. Leigh actually began her program in her basement in 2006. She began the Foster CARE Closet when she was a foster parent herself. Leigh had just taken three foster children into her home and had an immediate need for car seats, clothing, and baby items. As she began to gather these items, she came to realize that there were many other foster parents in the same situation as she was, lacking clothing and other items when children were placed into foster homes. As a result, Leigh found that many foster parents had to say no to taking placements into their home due to the inability to purchase necessities. Leigh was determined to find a better way to help these foster parents meet the tangible needs of the children while also focusing on the emotional needs of these children.

The Foster CARE Closet reaches out to all children who are wards of the state of Nebraska and provides free clothing and other necessary items. Since she first began the agency, Leigh worked to not grow too quickly as to not run out of funding, but the financial support came, and in 2011, more than 1,400 children were served throughout the state. Today, the Foster CARE Closet is located in a 3,200-square-foot building set up similar to any other clothing store.

Leigh's organization also supports families trying to negotiate a very difficult system as well as caseworkers and others working in the field. As Leigh says, "We offer support to the families by often serving as a buffer from an upset or angry foster parent and the caseworker. We spend countless hours helping caregivers understand the flow of a case and how to communicate effectively with a worker. We work hard with case managers to help them understand where there may be a misunderstanding between the caregiver and the worker. Sometimes just having that neutral party explain to the other how it feels can really help both sides move forward."

Along with this, the Nebraska-based Foster CARE Closet spends large amounts of time reaching out to the community in an attempt to educate others on the foster care system and the policies that go along with it. The nonprofit organization also strives to build positive relationships with others in the community, such as child placement agencies and others that serve families and children in need. Above all, according to Leigh, the Foster CARE Closet "offers hope to those who may feel that there is no other way for life to be" and that "we try very hard to be the hands and feet of God" (DeGarmo, February 2013-Clothing and Care: Helping Foster Children with Clothes, Support, & Love, *Foster Focus Magazine*). Well said, Leigh!

AGING OUT

One of the most heartbreaking and tragic parts about foster care is one much of our society does not have any idea about: aging out. Indeed, I have spoken to a large number of foster parents who truly do not understand how this process works, either. Yet for children in foster care who are approaching an age where they will no longer be part of the system, this transition is often a time of great confusion, sadness, and danger. At the same time, this transition can be a great opportunity for our churches to step forward and help God's children as they enter into an age of uncertainty.

Each year, between 20,000 and 25,000 foster children age out of the system and attempt to begin life on their own. Of the 500,000 children in care in the United States each year, this is a large and disturbing percentage. For many foster children, foster care is a temporary service before returning home to a parent, moving in with a biological family member, or even beginning a new life in an adopted home. Yet, for thousands who do not find reunification with family in their lives, reaching 18 years of age can be a tremendously frightening experience. For others, 21 is the year where they may find themselves no longer part of the foster care system, depending on the state.

For most young adults leaving home for the first time, they have someone to rely on when facing challenges, difficulties, and trials. Whether the problems are financial, emotional, school oriented, or simply a flat tire that needs to be fixed, most young adults can pick up a phone and call an adult who is quick to help. Foster children who age out of the system many times do not have this type of support: no one to call, no one who can come to their aid, no one to pray for them. Foster children who age out of the system face an array of problems and challenges. As you know and have probably witnessed, too often these children have already faced such hardships as neglect, abuse, learning disabilities, and abandonment. Along with these challenges, the majority of foster children have difficulties with school, with more than 50 percent of those who age out dropping out of school. In fact, only 2 percent of all foster children who age out of the foster care system graduate from college. That statistic is disturbing. Lack of financial skills, work experiences, social skills, and various forms of training, along with the lack of support from family and caring adults, makes aging out even more problematic.

As a result of these obstacles and challenges, most foster children who age out of the system find themselves at risk in several ways. To begin with, when foster children leave the foster care system, they often have no place to call home. As they struggle with financial problems, finding a safe and stable place to call home is hard. Too many foster children are forced to turn to the streets for a time. If they are fortunate, they may end up in a homeless shelter, but this situation is often not the case. In fact, over half of all youth who age out of the system experience homelessness in their young lives while 75 percent will end up in jail.

Former foster girls who have aged out of the system also have an increased risk of pregnancy, and many young men who age out of the system unexpectedly find themselves fathers and unable to properly provide for their child. These experiences are a cycle many foster teens continue as they repeat what their parents went through.

Recent studies have found that adults who spent time in foster care also suffer from the ravages of posttraumatic stress disorder. This disorder is so widespread among former foster children that it doubles the rate of U.S. combat veterans who suffer from it (DeGarmo-2015, Helping Foster Children in School, JKP). Indeed, many youth who leave foster care suffer from a number of mental health disorders, including depression, high anxiety levels, and mental illnesses. Drugs and substance abuse problems run rampant as well. Along with these health concerns, large numbers of these young adults don't have proper health care or insurance as they lose the coverage that was provided for them while in care. Many simply do not have someone to care for them when they fall sick or face medical emergencies.

There are ways that the church can help these young adults after they have aged out of foster care. Chief among them is mentoring. There are many organizations across the United States that offer opportunities to serve as a mentor. Mentoring provides former foster children not only a listening ear as they discuss the many challenges that they face but also wisdom and guidance during times of struggle. Along with this help, mentors can also act as prayer partners with the former foster youth and perhaps help lead the teen to developing a relationship with Christ. With as little as an hour a week, church volunteers and mentors can help foster children with many important life and social skills, while at the same time creating stable, positive, and healthy relationships, perhaps for the first time ever for the young adult. What a wonderful way to answer God's call to care for the least of these without being a foster parent itself.

Research has shown that most foster children struggle with academics while in school. After-school and college tutoring programs help those who have aged out learn not only the material being studied but also stronger study skills. As many aged out foster youth cannot afford school, assistance in this manner is most helpful. Communities can begin a foster scholarship fund or donate school supplies to local foster care agencies. These supplies can include paper, pencils, pens, calculators, backpacks, and other school needs. For those former foster children who are enrolled in college, bookstore gift cards and certificates can also be quite beneficial.

Along with school supply donations, former foster children have a great need for household goods. Clothes, cooking and bedding items, electrical appliances, furniture, and other household items can be donated to local foster care agencies. In fact, you can even contact your local foster care agency and inquire about being a transporter, providing transportation to aged out youth. As most former foster children struggle with money, it is likely that they will not have a car or any means of transportation. Volunteers can help by providing transportation to job interviews, school venues, and medical appointments.

For those businesses that wish to assist aged out foster children, discounts on services and goods are most helpful. Whether it is clothing, groceries, computers, phones and other electronic devices, medications, and even legal and financial services, discounts on these products and services can help those former foster children who struggle financially. Those who own a business may also wish to consider hiring former foster children and training them with the skills that fit the particular business.

Perhaps the biggest impact you can have is to be an advocate for change. By contacting lawmakers, politicians, and publicity agents through emails, letters, phone calls, or in person, one can bring attention to the needs of these young adults who face a series of challenges after leaving the foster care system. Advocates of change can also post information in editorial letters, websites, public forums, and so forth. By lobbying for change, new laws can be introduced and information can be brought forward to the general public.

EILEEN'S STORY

As Christians, we believe that God gives each of us spiritual gifts and special abilities that are to be used in the ministry of the church.

Paul wrote in 1 Corinthians 12 that there are different kinds of gifts, but the same spirit distributes them and that there are diversities of activities, but it is the same God who works all in all.

No matter what our interests, talents, and special abilities are, there is a place at our church for each person who wants to help our church realize its vision. Some choose to become mentors with the county's mentor program. Others serve with the local community food bank, and many participate with helping needy families with Christmas distributions.

While most of us were not given the gifts and commitment that it takes to become foster parents, many of us can help to facilitate a special place, a "safe haven" at the church where foster children can meet twice a month with their birth families.

Those of us who work with the support group Safe Havens are parents, grandparents, counselors, teachers, or nurses who are or have been in a profession relating to helping others. We all find it gratifying and fulfilling to play a very small role in this enormous system of foster parenting.

As a teacher with many years of experience in working with at-risk children, I always considered teaching as a way of serving God and putting into use the unique abilities and gifts that He graciously bestowed upon me.

It has been said that "when one door closes, another opens." Upon my retirement, God extended my calling and provided me with a place to continue serving children and families through my association with Safe Havens and the foster family dinners that our church provides during the school year.

How Faith Has Changed
Foster Children

As foster parents, we have the opportunity to be witnesses of God's great love for children, as well as His redeeming grace, mercy, and forgiveness. We can share our faith with these children and be His hands and feet, working for His glory to help children in need and planting the seed of faith in them.

Remember, though, that the seeds we plant may not bloom until years later. I often remind the foster parents with whom I work that it may take some time for the seeds of faith that they planted to bloom and blossom. Perhaps you feel that you are not making a difference in the lives of the children you foster. Perhaps you believe the work you do won't matter in the long run. Let me correct you, please. I want you to understand that what you are doing does matter, and it matters significantly.

There is a good chance that in the future, the foster child you cared for may not remember your name. There is a good chance that in the future, the foster child you care for may not remember your face. But I can assure you, each foster child who comes through your home will remember one thing: that for a period in his life, he was loved, and some day down the road, he will blossom into something better because of it. When you share your faith and God's love with a child in need, you are changing the life of a child and changing the world. You are answering God's call to serve Him and His children in need.

Through the years, I have met many former foster children, foster alumni who shared with me how God's grace changed their lives. Sometimes, these children learned about God's love from biological parents and birth family members before they came into care. Other times, they may have experienced God's grace and mercy from the foster parents who cared for them. Still other times, they may have realized God's power of love after they aged out of care. For many of these children, their faith may be the only thing to cling to for strength during times of tragedy, pain, and confusion. I am both delighted and honored to share some of these stories of faith from some alumni with you.

Esther's Story

I was born in St. Louis, Missouri, to a mentally-ill woman named Myrtle and to a man 20 years her senior named John Blazer. I was the second of three children born to my mother. My parents were indigent, and story has it that at one point they fed me syrup water just to keep me alive, but still, I was admitted to the hospital for malnutrition in spite of their best efforts.

Sixteen months later they would have another child together, and my father was forced to make the most horrific decision. Which child to keep and which one to give away? Back then, they didn't have government assistance programs as they do now, and even so, many were unable to swallow their pride enough to accept what help they could receive because it went against their beliefs. When I was about 20 months old, my mother had a "nervous breakdown." At this point, my father and mother divorced and my older brother and I entered into foster care.

I have only a few fear filled memories of this time in my life. In one vivid memory, my brother and I are in a cold, concrete, poorly lit room facing two women. I remember being consumed with terror and clinging to my brother's leg as I earnestly begged the two women, if only in my mind, not to take my brother away from me.

The second and significant memory I have during the time we were in this same foster home is of me standing at the side of the lake watching the older kids swim, waiting for my turn.

Suddenly, it began to rain and so my patiently awaited turn was promptly canceled. I remember even as a two year old thinking to myself, "It's not fair . . ." I was overwhelmed with emotion. I don't think I would be exaggerating to say I threw my hands on my hips in exasperation. My first experience with injustice! According to my brother's memory, we were packed up and sent to our mother again after approximately two years; I would have been about four years old. I do recall a beating that left bruises all over my lower body when I lied against my brother. I received 60 swats with a belt that I can vividly remember counting.

Shortly before my childhood ended at six years old, I remember waking up to my mother's boyfriend sitting on top of her hitting her as she lay in the floor face up. I remember crying and begging him to stop. He finally did. The next morning I was tasked to clean up the mess their fight had left behind. Food thrown at each other was left where it landed, stuck to the floor, the stove, and the kitchen counter. The cockroaches that infested our home were boldly feasting on the evidence of the previous night's violence.

After a temporary stay with a neighbor while the state decided what to do with us, we went to Juvenile Hall. It seemed like *The Green Mile* as I walked as fast as my little legs could carry me, struggling to keep up with the adults through seemingly endless corridors. We had to be buzzed through several locked doors. Finally, we arrived at a large room with several other children who peered at my brother and me. Once again, as seems to be the most consistent memory of my childhood, I clung to my brother for protection and for courage. Looking back, I'm confident he was afraid too, yet he had no one to cling to. We then went into a room where we picked our clothes and underwear out of bins that we promptly changed into and then forfeited our personal clothes that were on our backs.

We were only to be in Juvenile Hall briefly, but I came down with the mumps, and so the entire wing was on lockdown. I was put into solitary: a room by myself, 24/7. My food was literally slid through a briefly opened door to me on a tray by a 16-year-old girl who shared dreams with me of being adopted before she had to shut the door and shut me away from human contact again. I watched other children play via a window that gave a cruel view onto the playground.

It was during my "isolation" of being made to stay alone in a room with only a bed that I had my God experience. I lay in bed and sang the songs I learned at Vacation Bible School right before we were taken away from my mother. Over and over I would sing "Jesus Loves Me" and spell it out on the wall beside me. I would sing, "This little light of mine, I'm gonna let it shine." I vividly remember singing this song with conviction and would mean every syllable. I was determined that I would not let Satan blow out my light. One day I was overwhelmed with missing my mother as I tried to distract myself playing with my George Washington family paper dolls. My songs were not working on this particular day, either. I finally relented and broke down sobbing, aching for my mama. I lay on my side pretending in my mind that she was lying next to me. I tried to remember what she smelled like. I grew angry and frustrated when I could not wish my mother to me. I cried out to God at six years old and challenged Him, in a sense. I told Him that if it were true He was everywhere, that since my mother couldn't be there, then I needed Him to hold me since she couldn't. I remember a warmth sweeping over me in combination with a peace—and I drifted sweetly to sleep. God has forever been real to me and the one consistent presence in my entire life. I did not really know what He was all about, but I simply believed.

Today I am a proud war veteran, a registered nurse who works with high-risk pregnant women, an author, a songwriter, a crime fighter/victim advocate, and most recently, cofounder of Fostering SuperStars. My life is incredible and full of so many amazing, inspirational people. Do I still have triggers and moments that tempt me to relive and revisit dark places? Yes. But thanks to the many seeds of kindness that were planted in my life by people who not only talked about God but were the very arms and hearts of God for me when I was a traumatized, sad child—I made the choice to own and control my life by choosing to focus on my future instead of my past.

We have absolutely no control or input as to how we start this life, but we have everything to do with how we finish it. I believe

I am made in the image of God—so what does that tell me? All things are possible.

Drusilla's Story

The cookie jar sat on the counter. It was open. The cupboard above it was locked. "She forgot," I happily told my special Friend. I pulled the kitchen stool over, climbed up, grabbed a handful of cookies, and stuffed them in the pocket of the light jacket I wore. My dog, Shooey, ate one as I gobbled down the rest. His bulk and the shadows of the rose bushes that climbed the green lattice concealed me from the woman who sat reading near the playhouse and the other children as they ran about. The sugar left my mouth parched. I returned to the kitchen for a glass of water. The cookie jar still sat open on the counter. I grabbed another handful, carefully replaced the stool, took the cookies to the room I shared, and ate them as I read Johanna Spyri's *Heidi*. After drinking another glass of water from the bathroom, I walked back through the kitchen. Still, the cookie jar remained on the counter. I pocketed another handful and shared them with Shooey under the porch. Twice more, I walked through the kitchen and took more cookies. Then the jar was empty.

"Who ate all the cookies?" the woman demanded. Twelve children sat around the dining table or in chairs pushed against either long wall of the room. The woman waved her arms excitedly, "I can't believe this! I go in to make dinner and all the cookies are gone. Whoever ate the cookies confess! Right now!" I remained silent. "If no one confesses, I'll punish all of you." No one spoke. "Eve! Follow me."

She led Eve into the little parlor and closed the door. The sound of smacking resonated through the small glass panes on either side of the door. Eve's voice cried, "I didn't do it! I didn't do it!"

Soon, the woman's voice sounded, "Send Gerard in!" Eve came back through the parlor door. "Gerard," she sniffed. "It's your turn." Gerard disappeared behind the closed door. "Whoever ate those cookies had better confess," she demanded angrily, her face puffy, red, and wet with tears. "It's not fair that I should be punished! I didn't eat them!" I remained silent. Each child disappeared in turn behind the parlor door and returned crying, loudly demanding the culprit confess. My stomach seemed to sink down to my toes. I sat sideways on my chair hiding my face in the hard upholstered back. The youngest child in the house at the time, I was called last. A lump filled the back of my throat. I closed the parlor door behind me.

"I know you didn't take them," the woman spoke softly. "I'll spank the piano bench and you cry." She hit the upholstered surface. I howled. "You'd better run upstairs or they'll see you're not crying," she told me after smacking the bench several times. I covered my face with my hands and ran up the steps to the room I shared.

Gerard cried out, "Whoever took the cookies had better confess."

"They deserved it," I told my Friend as I sat on the window seat and hugged the eyeless bear. "Besides," I continued, "They hit me. And pinch me. And hurt me. And call me names 'cause I don't look like them or sound like them, 'cause I'm slow. You know the horrible things the boys do to me?" The warm, gentle tingle of my Friend's hug filled me. "Even Eve does those things to me! I hate them. They should be punished." The well within me gushed over, "She won't give me anything to eat. Neither will he. She always gives them things they can eat. I hate being hungry."

Before they sent me away from the violence that had invaded our lives, my grandparents had told me that God would take care of me. Our lives were steeped in faith. How could I not believe them? Death had taken my family, but I was never alone. My Friend, God, was always with me, accompanying me. My physical senses have always been intensely aware of Him, on the verge of touching, smelling, and even seeing Him. He has always been absolutely clear to the eyes of my heart. Even before I heard His voice, I understood. No matter what the man, the woman, and the other children in that house did to me, my Friend was with me helping me through the madness of those 11 years. And He is with me now.

Amy's Story

Ever live in a home where you were abused and scared for your life? But then on Sundays and Wednesdays during church service and Bible study, you had to act as though nothing was wrong, especially since your father was a deacon in the church and your mother was a Sunday School teacher? This was my life. Growing up, I use to hate church and God because church was supposed to keep me safe. Instead it let me down. Because after church, I would have to go back home and wait until that belt or blow to my body would come from my father. I used to also wonder, how could my father preach on love but then show no love at home? Nothing but hurt was displayed.

Once I was removed from my home and placed into the foster care system, I went through 16 foster homes over the course of being in care. Out of those 16 foster homes, I remember being with two foster parents who showed true love through how they treated me as a part of their home and displayed their love for God 24/7. Not just during church! Due to their modeling of God's love, I began to work on loving God and knowing He did love me. This allowed me to grow in love with God and model this same love for God to my foster children who enter into my home. Over the course of being a foster parent, I would have those moments of "when these children are removed from my home, how am I going to handle the loss?" But then it hit me, as long as I sow love into them and display the love of God on a daily basis, once they leave my home to reunify with biological parent(s), adoption, relative placement, or other arrangements, I know I did my part. And that love will never depart from them.

Ereka's Story

Wow! Who would have thought that being adopted was the best thing that could have ever happened? It wasn't always like that in the beginning . . . as a child, I didn't always quite understand. I remember sneaking away to read my baby book for comfort; it had all the information I needed. I felt abandoned. I felt no one cared. I felt "different" and disconnected from the world. My family did their very best to make me feel loved; however, I struggled with identity. Having a strong faith in God got me through some really tough times. I would cry a lot! However, I always felt some type of connection with God when I would stray away and cry off in a corner after something bad happened. As an adult, I appreciate those tough times because they molded me into something special, and now I use my story to inspire thousands! We must remember that everything happens for a reason and a season, but if we put our trust in our faith and God, He will always order our steps into the right place at the right time.

Davina's Story

My early memories of Illinois begin with the fear of going to sleep. I lived in fear due to the reoccurrence of being abused. Yet I innocently trusted everybody. It was a thin line between who I feared most—the man who abused me or the people who constantly flowed through our home to purchase drugs. I remember living in a shelter for abused women for a period of time. We also spent an entire summer in a hotel. This is where I felt most safe and secure. I was able to have a warm bed, take a hot shower, and watch cartoons like other kids my age

My oldest sister was placed in foster care a year prior to the rest of us being separated. She had a mandated court hearing scheduled. This process was to give our parents an opportunity to demonstrate to the court that they had the ability to provide for and protect the child in question. My mother never showed up for my sister's hearing. We were told she did not come because she could not drive. This prompted more action by social services. They soon came for me and my other two sisters. The day of separation was the most difficult of my life. I was now considered a ward of the state. When I arrived at my new foster home, I quickly learned my foster mother ran a tight ship. The house was packed with foster children.

I want you to imagine a shy eight-year-old girl displaced from her family. With poor eyesight and thick glasses, she is definitely not the picture of the outgoing woman I have since become. Because of my eye problems, those chunky, pink glasses became a constant fixture on my face. I hated wearing them, and the other children at school only made me feel worse. They would call me names and knock them off of my face so that I couldn't see. Bullying is always a horrible experience for a child. I blame my poor eyesight for having to repeat the third grade.

The memories I have of my third grade teacher still stick out in my mind. She was an absolute angel in my life. She would stay after school to help me with my homework. I still remember the multiplication and flash cards. When I felt frustrated, I would cry. This wonderful teacher would always lift my spirits by encouraging me and insisting that I was capable. Thinking back, she was the first person I felt ever really believed in me.

One evening, an evangelist came to our church. His message is still clear in my mind: God answers the prayers of those who believe. So in silence, I closed my eyes and prayed to the Heavenly Father to please restore my eyesight. I prayed for Him to make me "normal" so I would no longer need to wear glasses. Upon opening my eyes, I immediately noticed something different. My eyes had been healed!

My foster mother took me again to the same ophthalmologist who had prescribed those thick, ugly glasses. He had no explanation for the change in my eyesight. It did not matter to me how it happened, I just knew my eyes were normal and my heart was filled with joy and excitement. I wanted to run and tell everyone about my eyesight. I had faith the size of a mustard seed, and now I could see! I am now able to live my life with perfect vision. That childlike faith continued to help me though some very challenging times.

Life in a foster home was unstable. You never knew when or if you were going to be moved. In my foster home, we constantly had new children coming and going. When I did something wrong, I would worry and hope they didn't move me. I would go to my room and cry, worried and scared that I would be next.

On October 16, 1995, my fifteenth birthday, a CT scan showed a tumor in the back of my head on my cerebellum. We were sent to other doctors, only to be given the devastating news that my tumor was inoperable. We were told it was a life-threatening situation, and yet there wasn't anything anyone could do. Then on Thanksgiving Day, we received a miracle call. A doctor in St. Louis said he would take a chance and perform surgery to remove the tumor . . . the next morning!

I spent a couple days in ICU. I had stitches from the back of my head down to my neck. Although the surgery went well, my spirits were quickly shattered when I realized I would have to learn to walk again. I battled severe pain in the back of my head and still do at times. When I finally returned to school, the name-calling and the bullying returned full force. I felt like an outsider. I was repeatedly called a "retard." I decided to prove them wrong. I worked diligently to re-learn everything and achieved a huge milestone: I graduated from high school with the class of 2000! Everyone, with the exception of my special education teacher, said I would never be able to finish high school. Despite all the bullying and criticism, I defied the odds and was accepted into college and worked full time at the local hospital. I felt the pressure to make the right life decisions that would benefit my future. As I approached 18, I knew the foster care system was about to rid itself of me.

Yet despite it all, I've learned that God often has other plans for us. Just about everything I said that I would never do, God made happen. I got married, we have a child, and now I work as a national speaker to spread the word about how to improve the lives of young people in foster care. I'm an author and an expert on trauma-informed care. God has surely blessed me, and I continue to look to Him for all things.

SCRIPTURE VERSES
For Foster Parents

God's Call to Care for Children:

For I was hungry and you gave me something to eat, I was thirsty and you gave me something to drink, I was a stranger and you invited me in, I needed clothes and you clothed me, I was sick and you looked after me, I was in prison and you came to visit me.
—MATTHEW 25:35–36

Learn to do good; seek justice, correct oppression; bring justice to the fatherless, plead the widow's cause.
—ISAIAH 1:17 (ESV)

And he took a child and put him in the midst of them, and taking him in his arms, he said to them, "Whoever receives one such child in my name receives me, and whoever receives me, receives not me but him who sent me."
—MARK 9:36–37 (ESV)

He has shown you, O mortal, what is good. And what does the LORD require of you? To act justly and to love mercy and to walk humbly with your God.
—MICAH 6:8

Whoever receives one such child in my name receives me, but whoever causes one of these little ones who believe in me to

SIN, IT WOULD BE BETTER FOR HIM TO HAVE A GREAT MILLSTONE
FASTENED AROUND HIS NECK AND TO BE DROWNED IN THE DEPTH OF THE SEA.
—*MATTHEW 18:5–6 (ESV)*

THEN CHILDREN WERE BROUGHT TO HIM THAT HE MIGHT LAY HIS
HANDS ON THEM AND PRAY. THE DISCIPLES REBUKED THE PEOPLE,
BUT JESUS SAID, "LET THE LITTLE CHILDREN COME TO ME AND DO NOT
HINDER THEM, FOR TO SUCH BELONGS THE KINGDOM OF HEAVEN."
AND HE LAID HIS HANDS ON THEM AND WENT AWAY.
—*MATTHEW 19:13–15 (ESV)*

RELIGION THAT GOD OUR FATHER ACCEPTS AS PURE AND FAULTLESS
IS THIS: TO LOOK AFTER ORPHANS AND WIDOWS IN THEIR
DISTRESS AND TO KEEP ONESELF FROM BEING POLLUTED BY THE WORLD.
—*JAMES 1:27*

GIVE JUSTICE TO THE WEAK AND THE FATHERLESS; MAINTAIN
THE RIGHT OF THE AFFLICTED AND THE DESTITUTE. RESCUE THE
WEAK AND THE NEEDY; DELIVER THEM FROM THE HAND OF THE WICKED.
—*PSALM 82:3–4 (ESV)*

GOD'S WORDS OF COMFORT AND STRENGTH:

"FOR I KNOW THE PLANS I HAVE FOR YOU," DECLARES
THE LORD, "PLANS TO PROSPER YOU AND NOT TO HARM YOU,
PLANS TO GIVE YOU HOPE AND A FUTURE."
—*JEREMIAH 29:11*

IF YOU ABIDE IN ME, AND MY WORDS ABIDE IN YOU,
YOU WILL ASK WHAT YOU DESIRE, AND IT SHALL BE DONE FOR YOU.
—*JOHN 15:7 (NKJV)*

AGAIN, TRULY I TELL YOU THAT IF TWO OF YOU ON
EARTH AGREE ABOUT ANYTHING THEY ASK FOR, IT WILL BE DONE FOR
THEM BY MY FATHER IN HEAVEN. FOR WHERE TWO OR THREE GATHER
IN MY NAME, THERE AM I WITH THEM.
—*MATTHEW 18:19–20*

AND WHATEVER YOU ASK IN PRAYER, YOU WILL RECEIVE, IF YOU HAVE FAITH.
—*MATTHEW 21:22 (ESV)*

Now faith is the assurance of things hoped for,
the conviction of things not seen.
—*Hebrews 11:1 (ESV)*

God's Word about Judging Others:

Judge not, that you be not judged. For with the
judgment you pronounce you will be judged, and with the measure
you use it will be measured to you. Why do you see the speck
that is in your brother's eye, but do not notice the log that is in
your own eye? Or how can you say to your brother, 'Let me take
the speck out of your eye,' when there is the log in your own eye?
You hypocrite, first take the log out of your own eye, and then you
will see clearly to take the speck out of your brother's eye.
—*Matthew 7:1–5 (ESV)*

Do not speak evil against one another, brothers. The one
who speaks against a brother or judges his brother, speaks evil
against the law and judges the law. But if you judge the law, you
are not a doer of the law but a judge. There is only one
lawgiver and judge, he who is able to save and to destroy.
But who are you to judge your neighbor?
—*James 4:11–12 (ESV)*

Therefore you have no excuse, O man, every one of you who
judges. For in passing judgment on another you condemn
yourself, because you, the judge, practice the very same things.
We know that the judgment of God rightly falls on those who
practice such things. Do you suppose, O man—you who
judge those who practice such things and yet do them yourself
—that you will escape the judgment of God?
—*Romans 2:1–3 (ESV)*

Judge not, and you will not be judged; condemn not,
and you will not be condemned; forgive, and you will be forgiven.
—*Luke 6:37 (ESV)*

God's Word about Forgiveness:

For if you forgive other people when they sin against you, your heavenly Father will also forgive you. But if you do not forgive others their sins, your Father will not forgive your sins.
—Matthew 6:14–15

Get rid of all bitterness, rage and anger, brawling and slander, along with every form of malice. Be kind and compassionate to one another, forgiving each other, just as in Christ God forgave you.
—Ephesians 4:31–32

Then Peter came to Jesus and asked, "Lord, how many times shall I forgive my brother or sister who sins against me? Up to seven times?" Jesus answered, "I tell you, not seven times, but seventy-seven times."
—Matthew 18:21–22

God's Word about Adoption:

God decided in advance to adopt us into his own family by bringing us to himself through Jesus Christ. This is what he wanted to do, and it gave him great pleasure.
—Ephesians 1:5 (NLT)

God's Word about Grief and Sadness:

Come to Me, all you who labor and are heavy laden, and I will give you rest. Take My yoke upon you and learn from Me, for I am gentle and lowly in heart, and you will find rest for your souls. For My yoke is easy and My burden is light.
—Matthew 11:28–30 (NKJV)

The LORD is close to the brokenhearted and saves those who are crushed in spirit.
—Psalm 34:18

Blessed are those who mourn, for they will be comforted.
—Matthew 5:4

Humble yourselves, therefore, under God's mighty hand, that he may lift you up in due time. Cast all your anxiety on him because he cares for you.
—*1 Peter 5:6–7*

So do not fear, for I am with you; do not be dismayed, for I am your God. I will strengthen you and help you; I will uphold you with my righteous right hand.
—*Isaiah 41:10*

For no one is cast off by the Lord forever. Though he brings grief, he will show compassion, so great is his unfailing love. For he does not willingly bring affliction or grief to anyone.
—*Lamentations 3:31–33*

Praise be to the God and Father of our Lord Jesus Christ, the Father of compassion and the God of all comfort, who comforts us in all our troubles, so that we can comfort those in any trouble with the comfort we ourselves receive from God.
—*2 Corinthians 1:3–4*

"He will wipe every tear from their eyes. There will be no more death" or mourning or crying or pain, for the old order of things has passed away.
—*Revelation 21:4*

ALABAMA
DEPARTMENT OF
HUMAN RESOURCES
Center for Communications
Gordon Persons Building
STE. 2104
50 NORTH RIPLEY ST.
MONTGOMERY, AL 36130
PHONE: (334) 242–1310

WEBSITE:
dhr.alabama.gov/services
/Foster_Care/FC_Children_
Teens.aspx

ALASKA
CENTER FOR
RESOURCE FAMILIES
815 SECOND AVE., STE. 101
FAIRBANKS, AK 99701
PHONE: (800) 478–7307

WEBSITE:
hss.state.ak.us/ocs/Pages
/fostercare

ARKANSAS
FOSTER PARENT
SERVICES
P.O. Box 1437, Slot S560
Little Rock, AR 72203–1437
Phone: (501) 682–1442

Website:
fosterarkansas.org

ARIZONA
DEPARTMENT OF
CHILD SAFETY
P.O. Box 6123
Site Code 940A
Phoenix, AZ 85005–6123
Phone: (877) 543–7633

Website: dcs.az.gov/services
/foster_care_and_adoption

CALIFORNIA
DEPARTMENT OF
SOCIAL SERVICES
744 P St.
Sacramento, CA 95814
Phone: (800) 543–7487

Website:
cdss.ca.gov/cdssweb
/Default.htm

COLORADO
DEPARTMENT OF
HUMAN SERVICES
1575 Sherman St.
Denver, CO 80203
Phone: (303) 866–5948

Website:
colorado.gov/cs/Satellite
/CDHS-Main/CBON
/1251575083520

CONNECTICUT
DEPARTMENT OF
CHILDREN AND FAMILIES
Commissioner's Office
505 Hudson St.
Hartford, CT 06106
Phone: (860) 550–6300

Website:
ct.gov/dcf

DELAWARE
DEPARTMENT OF
SERVICES
*for Children, Youth, and
their Families*
1825 Faulkland Rd.
Wilmington, DE 19805
Phone: (302) 633–2657

Website:
kids.delaware.gov/fs
/fostercare.shtml

DISTRICT OF COLUMBIA
CHILD AND FAMILY SERVICES AGENCY
200 I. St., SE
Washington, DC 20003
Phone: (202) 442–6100

Website:
cfsa.dc.gov

FLORIDA
DEPARTMENT OF CHILDREN AND FAMILIES
1317 Winewood Blvd.
Building 1, Room 202
Tallahassee, FL 32399–0700
Phone: (850) 487–1111

Website:
fosteringflorida.com
/index.shtml

GEORGIA
DIVISION OF FAMILY AND CHILDREN SERVICES
2 Peachtree St., NW
Ste. 18–486
Atlanta, GA 30303
Phone: (877) 210–5437

Website:
dfcs.dhs.georgia.gov/portal
/site/DHS-DFCS

HAWAII
DEPARTMENT OF HUMAN SERVICES
Hui Ho'omalu
1390 Miller St.
Room 209
Honolulu, HI 96813
Phone: (808) 586–5667

Website:
hawaii.gov/dhs/protection
/social_services/child_
welfare/Foster

IDAHO
DEPARTMENT OF HEALTH AND WELFARE
P.O. Box 83720
Boise, ID 83720–0026
Phone: (800) 926–2588

Website:
healthandwelfare.
idaho.gov/Children
/AdoptionFosterCareHome
/tabid/75/Default.aspx

ILLINOIS
DEPARTMENT OF CHILDREN AND FAMILY SERVICES
406 East Monroe St.
Springfield, IL 62701
Phone: (800) 572–2390

Website:
state.il.us/dcfs/foster
/index.shtml

INDIANA
DEPARTMENT OF
CHILD SERVICES
P.O. Box 7083
Indianapolis, IN 46207–7083
Phone: (888) 631–9510

Website:
in.gov/dcs/index.htm

IOWA
DEPARTMENT OF
HUMAN SERVICES
1305 E. Walnut St.
Des Moines, IA 50319–0114
Phone: (866) 448–4605

Website:
dhs.iowa.gov

KANSAS
DEPARTMENT FOR
CHILDREN AND FAMILIES
Office of the Secretary
555 S. Kansas Ave.
Topeka, KS 66603
Phone: (785) 296–3271

Website:
srs.ks.gov/agency/Pages
/AgencyInformation.aspx

KENTUCKY
CABINET FOR HEALTH
AND FAMILY SERVICES
Office of the Secretary
275 E. Main St.
Frankfort, KY 40621
Phone: (800) 372–2973

Website:
chfs.ky.gov

LOUISIANA
DEPARTMENT OF
CHILDREN AND FAMILY
SERVICES
627 N. Fourth St.
Baton Rouge, LA 70802
Phone: (888) 524–3578

Website:
dss.state.la.us

MAINE
OFFICE OF CHILD
AND FAMILY SERVICES
2 Anthony Ave.
Augusta, ME 04333–0011
Phone: (207) 624–7900

Website:
maine.gov/dhhs/ocfs

MARYLAND
DEPARTMENT OF
HUMAN RESOURCES
311 West Saratoga St.
Baltimore, MD 21201
Phone: (800) 332–6347

Website:
dhr.state.md.us
/blog/?page_id=4800

MICHIGAN
DEPARTMENT OF HEALTH
AND HUMAN SERVICES
Capitol View Building
201 Townsend St.
Lansing, MI 48913
Phone: (517) 373–3740

Website:
mi.gov/dhs/0,4562,7-124-
60126---,00.html

MISSOURI
DEPARTMENT OF
SOCIAL SERVICES
*Broadway State Office
Building*
P.O. Box 1527
Jefferson City, MO 65102–1527
Phone: (573) 751–4815

Website:
dss.mo.gov/cd/fostercare

MASSACHUSETTS
DEPARTMENT OF
CHILDREN AND FAMILIES
600 Washington St.
Boston, MA 02111
Phone: (617) 748–2000

Website:
mass.gov/eohhs/gov
/departments/dcf

MINNESOTA
DEPARTMENT OF
HUMAN SERVICES
P.O. Box 64244
St. Paul, MN 55164–0244
Phone: (651) 431–3830

Website:
mn.gov/dhs

MISSISSIPPI
DEPARTMENT OF
HUMAN SERVICES
750 N. State St.
Jackson, MS 39202
Phone: (800) 821–9157

Website:
mdhs.state.ms.us

NEBRASKA
DIVISION OF CHILDREN
AND FAMILY SERVICES
P.O. Box 95026
Lincoln, NE 68509-5044
Phone: (402) 471-9272

Website:
dhhs.ne.gov/children_family
_services/Pages/children
_family_services.aspx

NEVADA
DIVISION OF CHILD AND
FAMILY SERVICES
4126 Technology Way
3rd Floor
Carson City, NV 89706
Phone: (775) 684-4400

Website:
dcfs.state.nv.us

NEW HAMPSHIRE
DEPARTMENT OF HEALTH
AND HUMAN SERVICES
129 Pleasant St.
Concord, NH 03301-3852
Phone: (800) 852-3345

Website:
dhhs.nh.gov/dcyf/index.htm

NEW JERSEY
DEPARTMENT OF
CHILDREN AND FAMILIES
50 East State St.
2nd floor
P.O. Box 729
Trenton, NJ 08625-0729
Phone: (855) 463-6323

Website:
state.nj.us/dcf

NEW MEXICO
CHILDREN, YOUTH AND
FAMILIES DEPARTMENT
P.O. Drawer 5160
Santa Fe, NM 87502-5160
Phone: (800) 432-2075

Website:
cyfd.org

NEW YORK
OFFICE OF CHILDREN
AND FAMILY SERVICES
52 Washington St.
Rensselaer, NY 12144-2796
Phone: (518) 473-7793

Website:
ocfs.ny.gov

NORTH CAROLINA
DEPARTMENT OF HEALTH
AND HUMAN SERVICES
2001 Mail Service Center
Raleigh, NC 27699–2001
Phone: (919) 855–4800

Website:
ncdhhs.gov/childrenand
youth/index.htm

NORTH DAKOTA
DEPARTMENT OF CHILDREN
AND FAMILY SERVICES
600 East Blvd. Ave.
Department 325
Bismarck ND 58505–0250
Phone: (701) 328–2316

Website:
nd.gov/dhs/services/childfamily

OHIO
DEPARTMENT OF JOB
AND FAMILY SERVICES
30 E. Broad St.
38th Floor
Columbus, OH 43215–3414
Phone: (614) 466–1213

Website:
jfs.ohio.gov/ocomm
_root/0002OurServices.stm

OKLAHOMA
DEPARTMENT OF
HUMAN SERVICES
5905 N. Classen Ct.
Ste. 401
Oklahoma City, OK 73118–5940
Phone: (800) 376–9729

Website:
okdhs.org/services/foster
/Pages/FosterCareHome.aspx

OREGON
DEPARTMENT OF
HUMAN SERVICES
500 Summer St. NE
Salem, OR 97301–1067
Phone: (503) 945–5944

Website:
oregon.gov/DHS/children

PENNSYLVANIA
DEPARTMENT OF
HUMAN SERVICES
P.O. Box 2675
Harrisburg, PA 17105–2675
Phone: (800) 692–7462

Website:
dhs.pa.gov

RHODE ISLAND
DEPARTMENT OF
HUMAN SERVICES
Louis Pasteur Building
57 HOWARD AVE.
CRANSTON, RI 02920
PHONE: (401) 462–5300

WEBSITE:
dhs.ri.gov

SOUTH CAROLINA
DEPARTMENT OF
SOCIAL SERVICES
P.O. BOX 1520
COLUMBIA, SC 29202–1520
PHONE: (803) 898–7601

WEBSITE:
dss.sc.gov/content
/customers/index.aspx

SOUTH DAKOTA
DEPARTMENT OF
SOCIAL SERVICES
700 GOVERNORS DR.
PIERRE, SD 57501
PHONE: (605) 773–3165

WEBSITE:
ss.sd.gov/childprotection
/fostercare

TENNESSEE
DEPARTMENT OF
CHILDREN'S SERVICES
UBS Tower
315 DEADERICK, 10TH FLOOR
NASHVILLE, TN 37243
PHONE: (615) 741–9701

WEBSITE:
tn.gov/dcs/section
/foster-care-adoption

TEXAS
DEPARTMENT OF
FAMILY AND
PROTECTIVE SERVICES
701 W. 51ST ST.
AUSTIN, TX 78751
PHONE: (800) 233–3405

WEBSITE:
dfps.state.tx.us

UTAH
DEPARTMENT OF CHILD
AND FAMILY SERVICES
195 NORTH 1950 WEST
SALT LAKE CITY, UT 84116
PHONE: (801) 538–4100

WEBSITE:
dcfs.utah.gov

VERMONT
DEPARTMENT FOR
CHILDREN AND FAMILIES
280 State Dr.
Waterbury, VT 05671–1030
Phone: (800) 241–2131

Website:
dcf.vermont.gov

VIRGINIA
DEPARTMENT OF
SOCIAL SERVICES
801 E. Main St.
Richmond, VA 23219–2901
Phone: (800) 552–3431

Website:
dss.virginia.gov/family/fc
/index.cgi

WASHINGTON
STATE DEPARTMENT
OF SOCIAL AND
HEALTH SERVICES
P.O. Box 45130
Olympia, WA 98504–5130
Phone: (800) 737–0617

Website:
dshs.wa.gov/ca/general
/index.asp

WEST VIRGINIA
BUREAU FOR CHILDREN
AND FAMILIES
350 Capitol St.
Room 730
Charleston, WV 25301
Phone: (304) 558–0628

Website:
dhhr.wv.gov/bcf/Pages
/default.aspx

WISCONSIN
DEPARTMENT OF
CHILDREN AND FAMILIES
201 East Washington Ave.
Second Floor
Madison, WI 53708–8916
Phone: (608) 267–3905

Website:
dcf.wisconsin.gov

WYOMING
DEPARTMENT OF
FAMILY SERVICES
2300 Capitol Ave.
Third Floor
Hathaway Building
Cheyenne, WY 82002
Phone: (307) 777–7561

Website:
dfsweb.state.wy.us/protective
services/foster-care/index
.html

RESOURCES:
National Organizations

ADOPTING.ORG

Information and resources for those considering becoming foster parents, for foster parents, and for those who were formerly fostered. Support, training, counsel for money issues, transitions, and practical help.

WEBSITE: adopting.org

NATIONAL FOSTER PARENT ASSOCIATION

National Foster Parent Association
1102 PRAIRIE RIDGE TRAIL
PFLUGERVILLE, TX 78660
PHONE: (800) 557–5238
FAX: (888) 925–5634

WEBSITE: nfpaonline.org
EMAIL: Info@NFPAonline.org

RESOURCES:
FAITH-BASED ORGANIZATIONS

AMARIS MINISTRIES

Amaris Ministries is a nonprofit ministry that cares for women, children, and families in their time of need by providing guidance, basic support, and information on adoption and foster care.

585 W. ORANGE AVE.
EL CENTRO, CA 92243
AMARISMINISTRIES.COM

AMG INTERNATIONAL

AMG International is an evangelical Christian missionary agency ministering in more than 30 countries of the world. Their numerous ministries include the AMG childcare centers, where thousands of hungry children are fed and cared for.

6815 SHALLOWFORD RD.
CHATTANOOGA, TN 37421
AMGINTERNATIONAL.ORG

ARROW CHILD AND FAMILY MINISTRIES

Arrow is a Christian provider of child welfare and educational services connecting churches and governments to serve vulnerable children and families.

2929 FM 2920
SPRING, TX 77388

ARROW.ORG

BAIR FOUNDATION

The Bair Foundation provides Christ-centered quality care and services dedicated to the treatment, restoration, and empowerment of children, youth, and families.

241 HIGH ST.
NEW WILMINGTON, PA 16142

BAIR.ORG

BETHANY CHRISTIAN SERVICES

Bethany Christian Services is a global nonprofit organization that strengthens families by providing adoption and foster care services, pregnancy and family counseling, and refugee and immigration services.

901 EASTERN AVE. NE
GRAND RAPIDS, MI 49503

BETHANY.ORG

CHRISTIAN FAMILY CARE AGENCY

Christian Family Care Agency is a private nonprofit social services agency that provides adoption, foster care, pregnancy counseling, and child and family counseling programs focused on meeting the needs of children and families in Arizona.

CFCARE.ORG

FAITHBRIDGE FOSTER CARE

FaithBridge Foster Care bridges the gap between those who need help and those who provide help.

2655 NORTHWINDS PKWY.

ALPHARETTA, GA 30009
FAITHBRIDGEFOSTERCARE.ORG

FOCUS ON THE FAMILY

Focus on the Family is a global Christian ministry dedicated to helping families thrive by providing help and resources for couples to build healthy marriages that reflect God's design and for parents to raise their children according to morals and values grounded in biblical principles.

8605 EXPLORER DR.
COLORADO SPRINGS, CO 80920–1051
FOCUSONTHEFAMILY.COM

FOSTER CARE CLOSET

The Foster CARE Closet is the only organization in the state of Nebraska organized to serve the large numbers of youth in the foster care system by providing quality clothing at no cost.

643 S. 25TH ST.
STE. 8
LINCOLN, NE 68510
FOSTERCARECLOSET.ORG

FOSTER CLOSET

The Foster Closet is a free resource for Northeast Florida's foster parents, relative, non-relative placements, and independent living teens to access clothing, children's accessories, toys, furniture, and more.

8307 BEACH BLVD.
JACKSONVILLE, FL 32216
FOSTERCLOSET.ORG

HOMES OF HOPE FOR CHILDREN

Homes of Hope for Children serves children in crisis throughout Mississippi by providing a campus of strong, Christian homes.

344 HAROLD TUCKER RD.
PURVIS, MS 39475
HOHFC.ORG

LIFELINE CHILDREN'S SERVICE INC.

Lifeline Children's Services is a full-service adoption and orphan care ministry serving families and children in the United States and around the globe.

2104 ROCKY RIDGE RD.

BIRMINGHAM, AL 35216

LIFELINECHILD.ORG

LIVING 1:27

Living 1:27 is a foster care ministry within the North Metro Atlanta church community that encourages families to step into foster care and equips them with a support network.

480 W. CROSSVILLE RD.

ROSWELL, GA 30075

LIVING127.COM

OLIVE CREST

Olive Crest is dedicated to preventing child abuse, treating and educating at-risk children, and preserving the family.

2130 E. FOURTH ST.

STE. 200

SANTA ANA, CA 92705

OLIVECREST.ORG

THE ORANGE DUFFEL BAG INITIATIVE

The Orange Duffel Bag Initiative is a nonprofit organization that provides educational and support programs to at-risk teens and young adults.

1801 PEACHTREE ST. NE

STE. 300

ATLANTA, GA 30309

THEODBI.ORG

PROJECT 1.27

Project 1.27 inspires, recruits, and equips churches and families to foster and adopt local children.

2220 S. Chambers Rd.
Aurora, CO 80014
PROJECT127.COM

PROMISE686
Promise686 equips churches and families to meet the needs of orphans and foster children by providing financial assistance, community support, and education with the goal to inform the community and reduce barriers to adopting and fostering.
4729 Peachtree Industrial Blvd.
Ste. 100
Berkeley Lake, GA 30092
PROMISE686.ORG

ROYAL FAMILY KIDS
Royal Family KIDS is the nation's leading network of camps and mentor clubs for children of abuse, abandonment, and neglect.
3000 W. MacArthur Blvd., Ste. 412
Santa Ana, CA 92704
ROYALFAMILYKIDS.ORG

TAPESTRY FAMILY SERVICES
Tapestry Family Services is a community-based nonprofit organization formed to develop and provide programs and services that support and advance the health and well-being of children with special needs and a high level of support for families—foster families, adoptive families, and birth families.
290 East Gobbi St.
Ukiah, CA 95482
TAPESTRYFS.ORG

TEEN LEADERSHIP FOUNDATION
Teen Leadership Foundation provides a safe haven and resource of support for young adults who have aged out of the foster care system. Additionally, they guide and equip churches and church leaders to provide mentor programs, leadership camps, youth groups, independent living skills, and housing.

P.O. Box 7342
NEWPORT BEACH, CA 92658
TEENLEADERSHIPFOUNDATION.COM

THE MENTORING PROJECT

The Mentoring Project exists to rewrite the fatherless story through mentoring. The Mentoring Project inspires, recruits, trains, equips, refers, and matches men and women to become relational youth mentors throughout North America and in targeted cities globally.
5319 SW WESTGATE DR. #237
PORTLAND, OR 97221
THEMENTORINGPROJECT.ORG

UNITED METHODIST CHILDREN'S HOME

The United Methodist Children's Home places children into safe and loving foster care homes while helping to restore family relationships. It also prepares and educates young adults still in Georgia's foster care system and strengthens and preserves families, by providing housing and support to families at risk of homelessness.
500 S. COLUMBIA DR.
DECATUR, GA 30030
UMCHILDRENSHOME.ORG

New Hope® Publishers is a division of WMU®, an international organization that challenges Christian believers to understand and be radically involved in God's mission. For more information about WMU, go to wmu.com. More information about New Hope books may be found at NewHopePublishers.com. New Hope books may be purchased at your local bookstore.

Use the QR reader on your smartphone to visit us online at NewHopePublishers.com.

If you've been blessed by this book, we would like to hear your story. The publisher and author welcome your comments and suggestions at newhopereader@wmu.org.

Know More Orphans

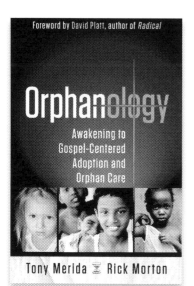

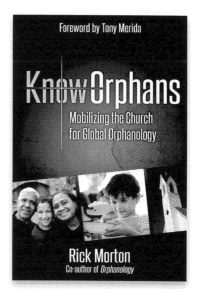

Orphanology

AWAKENING TO GOSPEL-CENTERED
ADOPTION AND ORPHAN CARE
Tony Merida & Rick Morton
ISBN-13: 978-1-59669-302-9
$14.99

Containing concrete ideas for
how Christians, their churches,
and groups of churches can
respond tangibly to God's
call to care for the fatherless,
Orphanology demonstrates how
adoption, foster care, and other
forms of orphan ministry are
accessible to every believer and
every church. It also introduces
innovative approaches to orphan
ministry including orphan hosting.

Know Orphans

MOBILIZING THE CHURCH FOR
GLOBAL ORPHANOLOGY
Rick Morton
ISBN-13: 978-1-59669-399-9
$14.99

In this provocative follow up
to *Orphanology*, author Rick
Morton provides the framework
for families and churches to have
a gospel-centered response
to the growing global issue of
orphan care. *KnowOrphans* is the
next step in conversation as this
evangelically-based movement of
orphan care matures and begins
to live out James 1:27 globally.